STACKING THE DECK

Secrets of the
World's Master
Card Architect

BRYAN BERG

with Thomas O'Donnell

A FIRESIDE BOOK
Published by Simon & Schuster
New York • London • Toronto • Sydney • Singapore

FIRESIDE
Rockefeller Center
1230 Avenue of the Americas
New York, NY 10020

FIRESIDE and colophon are registered trademarks
of Simon & Schuster, Inc.

For information regarding special discounts for bulk
purchases, please contact Simon & Schuster Special Sales
at 1-800-456-6798 or business@simonandschuster.com

Designed by Christine Weathersbee

Manufactured in the United States of America

10   9   8   7   6   5   4   3   2   1

Library of Congress Cataloging-in-Publication Data
Berg, Bryan.
    Stacking the Deck : secrets of the world's master card
architect / Bryan Berg with Thomas O'Donnell.
        p.   cm.
    "A Fireside book."
    1. Houses of cards (Playing card constructions) I. O'Donnell,
Thomas II. Title.
GV1218.C3B47 2003
795.4—dc21   2003045436

ISBN 0-7432-3287-9

To Grandpa Ray—BB

To Tony and Tommy—TRO

ACKNOWLEDGMENTS

Legions of people helped bring this book to life but especially some true friends who always went the extra mile. Cameron Campbell, Chad Veach, and Steve Crabb were substantial contributors, not only to this book but to countless other projects and circumstances—usually at the last minute. Their greatest contributions have been friendship and tolerance. They have been an inspiration for many years.

We also owe thanks to Mary Kay Shanley, Larry Lehmer, Steve Buttry, and Jonathan Kronstadt for the life-saving advice they gave as *Stacking the Deck* took shape. And we're grateful to the Science Center of Iowa for use of their facility.

We're especially thankful for the help of Sandra Choron, whose enthusiasm for this project rivaled our own.

—*Bryan Berg and Thomas O'Donnell*

CONTENTS

Start Stacking

People often use the phrase "house of cards" to describe something shaky and unstable. They haven't seen what I've been building with cards for eighteen years—miniature versions of stadiums, landmarks, and futuristic cities. I've set six Guinness World Records for the tallest freestanding house of playing cards.

Everything was built without folding, taping, gluing, notching, or otherwise joining any cards. Even so, my creations are incredibly strong. One of my structures supported 2,700 pounds of Las Vegas showgirls. Another held an entire Little League team—complete with coaches. It sounds impossible, but as you read this book you'll see it can be done.

This book will teach you to make strong, tall buildings that are also beautiful and, at times, whimsical. You'll become accomplished at techniques you never dreamed of. Or perhaps you'd rather just look over the stories and photos about the unbelievable things I've built.

Stacking: It's in the Cards

I'll soon show you how easy card stacking can be. Before you build, though, get the right cards and the right location.

♣ The best cards for building have standard thickness, standard size, and less than standard finish. Buy decks with a matte finish—not a slick, glossy coating. The cheapest playing cards often are the best for building. Look for decks wrapped in cellophane. I use Pla-Mor brand from United States Playing Card Company, but any inexpensive, uncoated cards will do. Make sure they're flat, and toss any bent or wrinkled cards. The photo shows some of the Pla-Mor styles. The designs may vary, and Pla-Mors may not be available in your area. If you have difficulty finding them, visit www.cardstacker.com to email me, or write me at the address at the end of this book.

♣ Business cards, index cards, or recipe cards will work instead of playing cards. I like regular playing cards, though, because it doesn't seem real without diamonds, hearts, clubs, and spades. When I first did this crazy hobby for money, I built towers with the backs facing out. I started putting the suits facing out because people kept asking me what they were.

♣ While old decks often have great surfaces, they're usually too beat up and bent or inconsistent to be useful.

♣ If you use multiple decks, don't even think of building with different-size cards. All the decks must be of consistent size and quality.

♣ Avoid sports cards. Their paper is too thick, and their finish is too glossy. The sports cards I've used usually were specially made for building.

Clear the Construction Zone

Choose your card-building surface carefully. It should be textured, like short carpet or a piece of particleboard. You could build on a table, but your structure might fall if the surface is bumped. The floor usually is the best place there is—but not in front of a blowing fan or an open window on a breezy day.

Other Tips

♣ In most cases, each card will lean gently against another. You'll be able to lean cards at a smaller angle as you become practiced in the art of card construction. But remember: Beginners will have a hard time controlling cards placed too close to vertical.

♣ If a card is crooked or isn't standing right, use the end of a spare card to nudge it into place. Big, clumsy fingers are more likely to knock down a bunch of cards than to fix a single one. A spare card also is useful for removing cards if a structure partially collapses. Use it like a shovel: Carefully pick up and scoop the cards off the undamaged part of the building.

♣ The cards in buildings pictured in this book may change from one photo to the next. That's usually because something fell down and had to be rebuilt. In fact, what you see here is probably only two-thirds of what I built for the book. The rest fell down. I'm not perfect; you shouldn't expect to be, either.

♣ Try to sit in a way that's comfortable without leaning on your building surface if it's a table or piece of board. Most of the photos in this book show me reaching in front and progressing away from me as I built. It might be easier for you to build toward yourself.

♣ Take it easy! Have fun! Building will be easier if you have relaxed, steady hands.

Put 'Em Up

The structures I'm about to demonstrate aren't perfect or fancy. They're designed to get you comfortable with cards. Don't worry for now about making everything exactly straight or just like the illustrations. We'll get more formal and organized later. Just experiment and learn the basics: the four-card cell that is the seed of life when it comes to card building.

Cards ready? Building area ready? Hard hat on? Let's do it.

1. Place the cards within easy reach. Lay the first card on its long edge; hold it upright and don't let go. You'll be building a box of four cards, and it could

collapse if you release this card before they're all in place. Use a second card to make a T by gently leaning it perpendicular to the first card.

2. Card 3 makes a second T when its middle is gently leaned against the end of card 2.

3. Complete the box. Lean card 4 against the end of card 3 so the end doesn't quite touch the card in your hand.

4. Carefully lean the card in your hand against card 4 and let go.

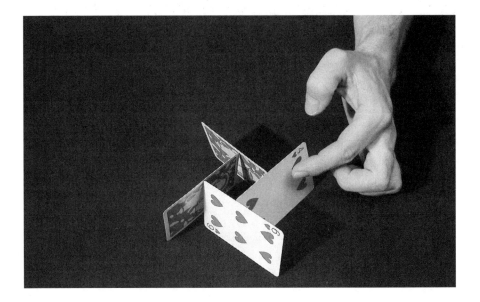

What you have now should look like a pinwheel, with a square in the middle and a tail extending from each corner. Unbelievably, this is the hardest thing to accomplish in card stacking—and the root of virtually everything else. If you can conquer these four steps, the rest is a cakewalk.

This central "cell" makes card buildings incredibly strong. I routinely build slightly more complex one- or two-story card buildings that support at least five concrete blocks—more than 150 pounds. Architects often design skyscrapers the same way, with a strong concrete-and-steel core. It supports the floors so exterior walls can be made of lighter materials, such as glass.

Now you'll carefully place four cards on top of the box to make a roof.

1. Lay two cards next to each other atop the cell. Don't overlap them.

2. Lay two parallel cards on top, perpendicular to the first two. Again, don't overlap them. The roof should be two cards thick all around.

You've finished one "story" of your building. Savor the victory and prepare yourself for the next one—building a second story. While building on cards instead of carpet may seem tougher, cards are actually the perfect building surface.

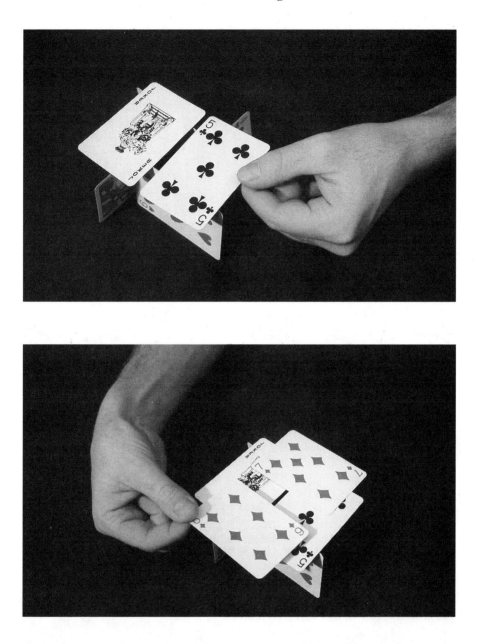

You'll follow the same steps used to build the first story.

1. Gently place the first card on its edge. You should try to put it in line with the "first-story" card below it, but don't worry too much about that. Hold the card upright and let it "float" between your fingers. You should

float this first card any time you're building on a roof. If you grip it, any slight movement will be transmitted to the cards beneath it, possibly damaging the first story.

2. Carefully place card 2 perpendicular to card 1 and lean it in to make a T.

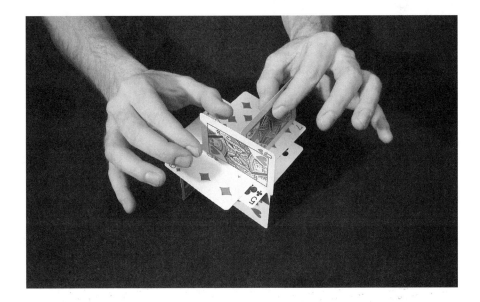

3. Lightly set the third card on its edge in the same way and lean it against the end of card 2.

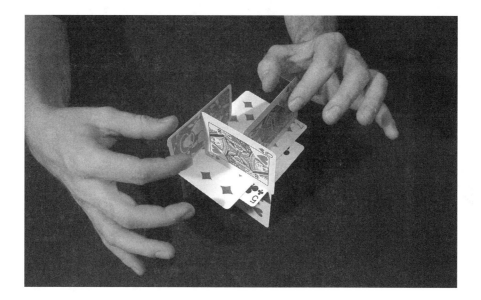

4. Set the fourth card perpendicular to card 3.

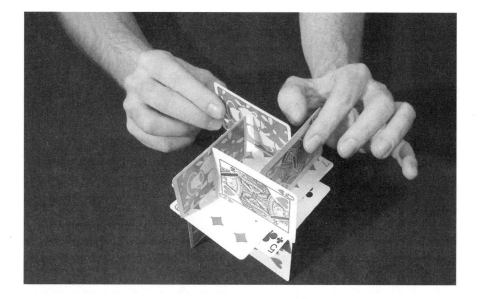

5. Gently lean the card in your hand against card 4 to complete the cell.

All that's left is to put on another roof.

1. Lay two parallel cards across the cell. Don't overlap them.

2. Lay two parallel cards on top, perpendicular to the first two. Again, don't overlap them.

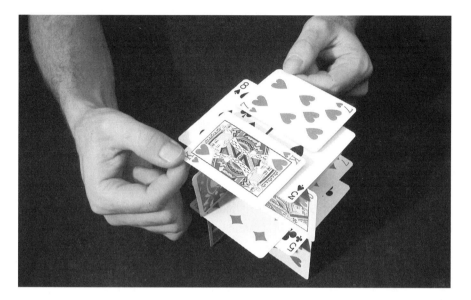

There's your two-story card building. With enough cards, you can add more stories in the same way until the whole thing implodes. As you get better at it, you'll start merging some steps or taking them a little out of order. Improvisation is the mark of a top card builder.

A Few Short Stacks

Now let's move on to a few easy buildings that will show how that four-card cell is the foundation that supports everything. None of these buildings should take long once you've mastered the basics, yet they all have pleasing architectural structures and even some decorations. Once again, don't worry about making these look just like the pictures. Yours could be more extensive or less extensive. Just get used to putting up the cards, and don't fret over the occasional collapse.

1. Start again with a basic four-card cell and lay a card perpendicular to one of the tails sticking out from it. Put a card perpendicular to that one, and another card perpendicular to that one for as far as you like, making a kind of crosshatch pattern. Don't worry about making complete cells. The cards will stay standing as long as the four-card cell you started with is there.

But take away one card from the cell, and the whole structure will collapse. That shows how the cell is the bulwark that supports everything.

2. Lay a roof over the cell: two pairs of cards layered at right angles to each other.

3. Lay a roof over the herringbone cards. Don't worry about the arrangement; just try to use small overlaps. The roof will help stabilize the structure by holding the cards in place.

4. Put another cell on the first layer, remembering to let the first card float between your fingers. Try to line it up with the cell below, but don't obsess over alignment.

5. Add a crosshatch pattern, as in the first layer, and roof it the same way.

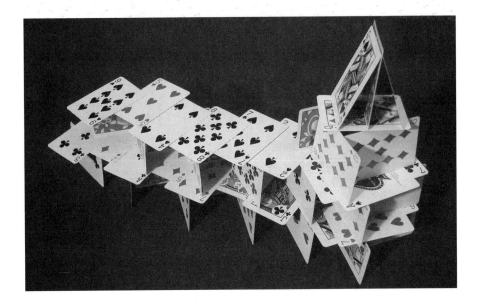

6. Put on a cell for the third story. Roof it with four cards, laid two abreast at right angles. You also could add a steeple for a final touch: Hold three cards on the work surface so that the outer two lean against the center card. Now move the steeple onto the structure and adjust the outer cards so they're balanced against the middle one.

You can make this building narrower and taller. The bottom layer of the structure has a cell supporting five cards in a crosshatch, a second layer of a cell and three cards, and a third layer of a cell with a single added card. The last two stories are single cells with a steeple on top.

This last structure drops the crosshatch pattern except for one card on the bottom grid. It's topped with five cells and a steeple.

Even these quick structures can be strong. Try putting one hand on the top and another under the floors and picking them up as a unit. Your friends won't believe it.

Towering Aspirations

- Record-setting tower
- Spirit Lake, Iowa, spring 1992
- 208 decks
- 40 hours

I'd have to try a hundred-foot tower to be as mystified now as I was when I built my first record-setter. It wasn't yet an intuitive thing for me to build something fourteen and a half feet tall, topping the previous record of twelve feet, ten inches. The biggest house of cards I'd ever built was around ten feet—and it was far from perfect.

John Franklin, an engineer I was working for in my hometown, heard about that one and learned that the world record was only a couple of feet taller. "What are you waiting for?" he asked. "If you can build ten feet, you can build more than twelve feet." I built a tower in his office that was just under the record.

I broke the record several weeks later—as part of a high school math project. My dad and I set up scaffolding in the school auditorium, and I scavenged an old piece of plywood for the base.

I bought a lot of cards and worked a lot of hours to build that silly little tower. I spent four days stacking. (Now I could get it done in one busy day.) I even spent the night as security guard for fear the tower might be sabotaged. The old building's clanking, hissing steam heat made the whole thing a spooky experience.

I wasn't sure how much weight the cards would hold, so I doubled or even quadrupled the thickness of cells in the bottom stories—especially the interior cards. I've since figured out that cards on the *edges* of each floor are the most vulnerable. Interior cards are braced in both of the directions in which they could fall or bulge. Edges are braced in only one direction. If a tower fails, it's most likely to happen on the perimeter.

That tower also was the slimmest of all my record-breakers. Big towers really are just lanky pyramids, rarely more than twelve times as tall as they are wide at the base. That first tower was fourteen feet, six inches tall but only fourteen inches square at the base, so it slightly violated that one-to-twelve ratio.

I also used fewer cards in the upper layers for fear their weight would crush the

bottom cards. I later decided that that's unnecessary: What difference does it make if it's the ninetieth floor? Since the floors get steadily smaller as the tower gets higher, there are only a few cards in the tallest floors anyway.

That first record-setter still seems huge to me, even though I've since built a tower almost twice as tall. It was probably the most risky tower I've built because it was so narrow. I haven't built one that skinny since.

Local radio stations and the Spirit Lake weekly newspaper documented the feat. Franklin and my math teacher both measured the tower and signed affidavits for Guinness. Then I knocked it down.

When I got the certificate designating me a world record holder, I felt like a rock star—and I got an A in math.

The Zen
of Card Stacking

I started card stacking while sitting on the lap of my grandfather Ray Trojahn in northern Iowa. When our family finished its heated tournaments of games such as 31 and Up and Down, Grandpa and I would see how tall we could build cards before they collapsed.

I'd keep trying when I got home. It was frustrating until I figured something out. If I carefully stood the cards in a series of boxes, like a grid or honeycomb, the buildings were stronger. They withstood even severe conditions—like my brother, Eric, purposely stomping around the house.

I was in high school when Eric's constant taunting set me on the path to a card-stacking career. Just to show him, I built a tower eight feet tall—about as high as I could go in my parents' living room. When I learned it was only four feet and change short of the world record, I set out to build an even taller tower. My first record-setter was seventy-five "floors" tall. When I built it in the Spirit Lake High School auditorium in 1992, I had no idea that someone might pay me to do it again.

The *National Enquirer* called two years later, when I was an architecture student at Iowa State University. Someone at the supermarket tabloid had seen me in the *Guinness Book of World Records,* and now the *Enquirer* wanted a story. Three days after the story appeared, *CBS This Morning* called. I soon built a tower fifteen feet, eight inches tall for the show. I was a professional card stacker—whatever that was.

Since then, I've traveled to trade shows, conventions, and fairs, building everything from stadiums like ALLTEL Stadium in Jacksonville, Florida, to landmarks like the Liberty Bell. I'm the "freak show" that attracts customers and spectators.

People say I must be weird to spend days piling one card on top of another and another and another, but card stacking is part of my interest in architecture and in how things go together. I graduated from ISU, and I teach architecture there now. I've found I appreciate buildings that are honest about their materials and structure—buildings that speak of how they're made. Architects don't hide the identity of these buildings. Grain bins and barns, for instance, can be beautiful because they state their purpose clearly through how they're made and what they're made of.

That's why I believe buildings are most beautiful when they're under construction. It's then that they display their true selves. That's when a building is most honest about its materials and structure.

Card buildings are like that: They rarely mask how they're made. It's clear they've been stacked and assembled into fantastic shapes. People appreciate them not only because the material is familiar but also because they've tried to make something similar. They'll stop to look because they see cards built extraordinarily tall, or they'll see a massive bowl or dome and believe the whole thing is impossible.

That's how good architecture should be. People value novel things. When they see a building that is fundamentally different, they'll stop to look. They'll tell their friends. Just as a good architect does, a great card stacker takes the ordinary—a deck of cards—and transforms it.

After I do demonstrations at schools, parents tell me that their children become engrossed in card stacking for weeks. "I wish my kids could find other interests that absorbed them like this," they say. Perhaps that's what this book really is about: falling in love with your interests and following them passionately throughout your life.

In this chapter, we'll take the simple towers you built in Chapter 1 and add to them. I'll show you how the cell structure is the DNA of card building. It's the vessel that makes it all work. I'll teach you to broaden that structure to make it bigger and bigger.

Now start building—and keep your big brother away.

Grid Crazy

I build grids—or what I also call waffles—everywhere. They include standard grids, with square cells, and offset grids, with bigger cells that make a pattern of large squares alternating with small rectangles.

Grids are cells strung together into rows. They can be challenging, because one falling card can bring down the entire waffle. The cards at the edges are the most likely to fall because they're braced in only one direction. If one falls, two other cards are no longer braced and also could fall, setting off a chain reaction. It still happens all the time to me, even after years of practice, so take heart.

To make a grid, start with a basic cell and lean cards perpendicular to the tails sticking out from it.

Keep crossing the cards you add to make more cells, moving first in one direction to get a row, then across again to make another row.

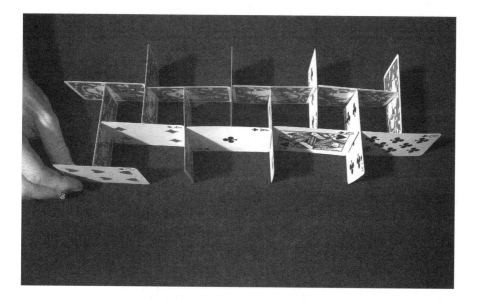

Grids can be whole- or half-card widths, measured at their widest points. This grid is four and a half cards wide by three cards deep.

Take away a row, and it's a four-card by two-and-a-half-card grid.

Grids are modular, but that doesn't mean they're inhibiting. With patience, you can make a grid whatever you want it to be. It's even possible to shift the size of the cells after a grid is built. Start by moving over cards in one row.

Then move the cards they support, one at a time.

Keep sliding cards in a row, one at a time, into the configuration you want. This grid is shifted across its width.

This grid has also been shifted from front to back. The result is a grid of wide cells alternating with smaller spaces.

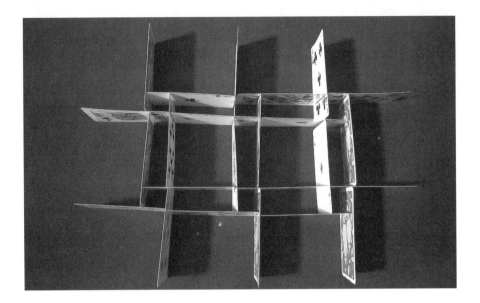

Of course, you can build a grid with offset cells rather than shift an already constructed grid.

Just cross the cards toward their ends instead of at their middles.

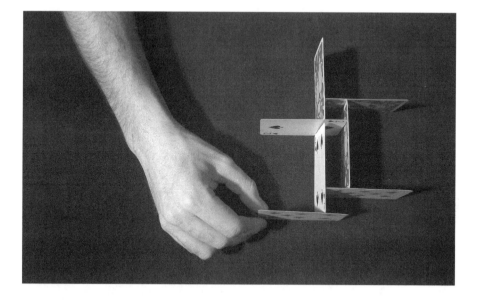

It's more difficult to do this, though, because you're no longer meeting the cards at their natural balance points.

It took me three tries to build this example of an extreme offset, in which the cards are placed just a fraction of an inch from their ends.

You might call this offset a migraine grid. It's artistic, but it's tricky—so tricky I'd probably use it only as a last resort. You'll use offset grids only when they must fit in a certain area. They also can make the edge of a grid look neat, even without a "fence" around it, because there's less tail protruding. Try offset grids sometime.

Take It Easy

Here's a grid-based building that's easy to throw together.

1. Make a broad grid—three and a half cards by four cards. Don't worry about making it precisely straight or exactly like the illustrations.

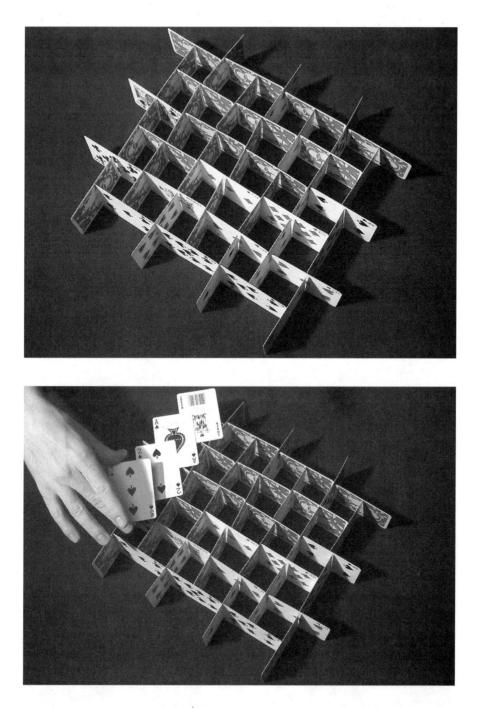

2. Now put on a roof. Place cards at an angle to the grid cells, starting at one corner and working across in one direction. Overlap them slightly.

3. Put on another row, overlapping it with the first. This herringbone pattern is one of my standard roofs. It ties the grid together and flattens out the ridges and high points that can accumulate when one grid is stacked atop another for several layers.

4. Start another grid atop the first one, remembering to float the first card between your fingers so the cards below it aren't disturbed.

5. Make this grid a card or half-card smaller each way than the first—two and a half cards by three cards. You needn't complete all the cells if there isn't room.

6. Put on another herringbone roof and start a third layer. Remember to float the first card. Don't worry about lining up with the grid below or keeping your rows perfectly straight.

7. Make the third grid a card or half-card smaller than the second—two cards by two cards.

8. Top it with a few cards in a herringbone pattern. You can stop there or keep stacking, with smaller grids on each layer until you're stacking single cells. I quit after five layers. If you can do better, you may be ready for the pros.

If you have a cat, try enticing it into demolishing your building. Here's what J.R. did to this structure.

This basic structure isn't as polished as the things you'll do later, but it's angular and attractive in its own right. It shows that mass—the weight of many cards—and repetition are the keys to successful buildings.

It's also about volume. I sometimes think of a big grid as a water tank I'm filling with cards. Each cell has volume. If it could be filled, it would hold water like an ice-cube tray. I've sometimes wondered how many gallons a grid would hold in all those spaces.

Bulking Up

Now take the skills you've learned and clean them up to make a truly strong card structure. This one took me about an hour and used a little more than one deck.

1. Start with a grid two cards square.

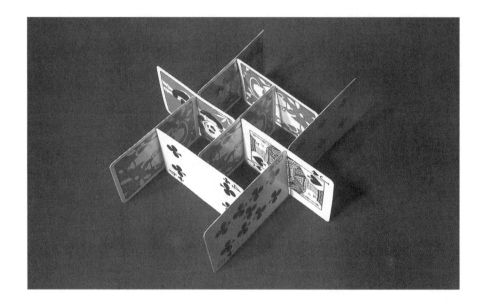

2. Put a "fence" on it by first leaning cards against the tails.

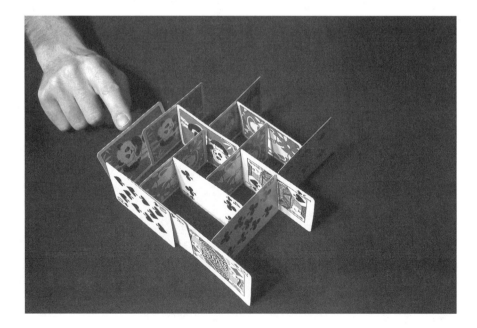

3. Overlap those cards until there is a solid wall on each side of the grid. This fence does nothing to make the building stronger, it only makes it look neater and provides support for the roof.

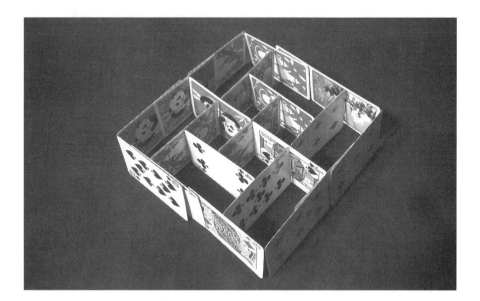

4. This time, use parallel cards to make the roof. Put three on each side (six cards total), hanging them over the edges slightly. Don't overlap.

5. Lay six more cards at right angles to the first six. The weight of twelve cards will help keep the grid in place.

6. Leave a hole in the roof where the cards cross in the center of the grid.

Start the second layer by aligning the first cards with the cards that are visible through the roof hole.

Remember to float the first card in your hand as you build the first cell.

1. Add cards to make a grid two cards across, identical to the first story.

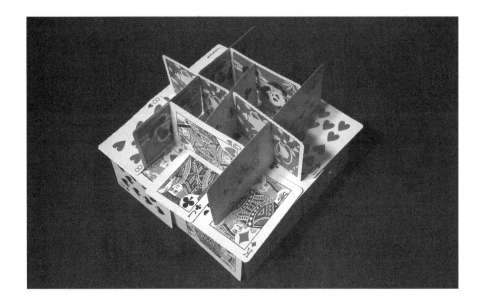

2. Then begin a fence by carefully leaning cards against the tails extending from the grid. Cover the gaps between those cards to make a complete wall.

3. Roof this grid with twelve cards again: three on each side and six more placed at right angles to the first six.

Now you're ready for a stress test. I piled this two-story building with unopened decks to test its strength. You'll make stronger buildings if you take care to align the grids. This structure used just 64 cards, but I piled 118 decks—more than 6,300 cards—on it before it collapsed. In theory, the building was strong enough to support nearly two hundred more layers.

Some grids can support even more weight. I built a three-foot-by-four-foot grid at the Science Center of Iowa in Des Moines in January 2002. I used three cards in each part of the cells; otherwise, the structure was essentially the same as the grids I just showed you.

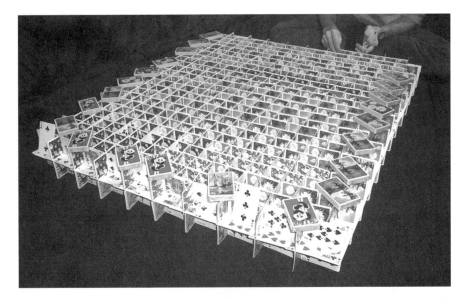

I laid three sheets of particleboard on the grid and started adding people. When I finally ran out of space, the grid was holding thirteen adults and children—more than 1,600 pounds when the particleboard was included. I believe it would have held at least another 1,000 pounds.

Pyramid Power

After you've built the structures in this chapter and experimented on your own, take a crack at this. It's designed to resemble a Mayan pyramid from Mexico. It took me a little over two hours and used about six decks. But first, here are some more tips for grid building:

♣ Grids are most likely to fail on the edges, where cards are braced in only one direction. To avoid that, temporarily lean cards against the edges. They're like the braces carpenters use to support frame walls until other walls support them.

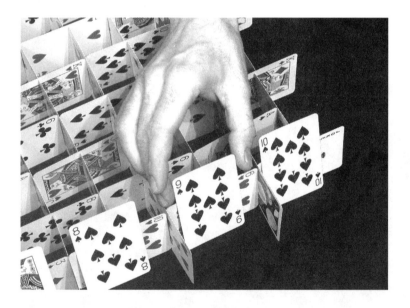

♣ You can pin down a grid by putting unopened decks on its edges.
♣ After you've gotten a few cells down in a large waffle, you can push in a bit on each new card you add, nudging the interior cards so they're completely upright. As you do so, put a finger on the card you're pushing against to keep it steady. Be careful, though: Push too hard and you could mangle the whole thing, turning cards at an angle or making them fall. You have to develop the confidence to know how hard to push.

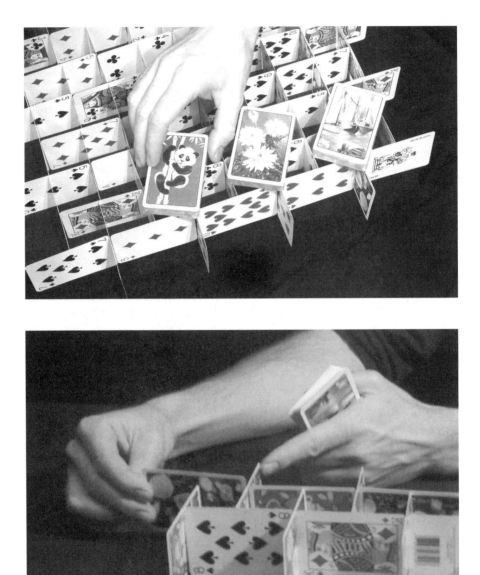

♣ Stop occasionally to nudge crooked cards back into line—but don't get obsessed about alignment.

♣ Try holding extra cards in your nondominant hand as you build. Unless you have small hands, this method shouldn't prevent you from building, and it keeps cards ready for use. Just don't grip them so tightly that they bend.

Now for the pyramid:

    1. Start with a standard grid, six cards wide on all sides.

    2. Begin the roof by laying cards lengthwise along the edges so they hang over slightly. Balance them across the tails sticking out from the grid.

3. Close the gaps between those cards with more cards. Overlap them slightly. This roof edge provides some extra weight atop the perimeter cards, making them less likely to fall.

4. When you're done, cards along its edges should frame the grid.

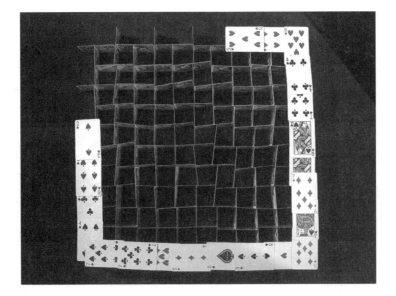

Now put on a herringbone roof. Start at a corner and lay cards across the grid at an angle, overlapping them slightly. Keep putting on cards so the rows also overlap slightly. Leave one spot near the center uncovered so you can see an intersection in the first grid. This will be a reference point to line up your second grid.

1. Align the second grid with the cards that are visible through the roof hole.

2. Remember to hold the first card loosely.

3. Continue building cells across the grid. Make this layer one card smaller than the first—down from six cards square to five cards square, so the empty edge re-creates the Mayan pyramid's stair-step structure. Then roof it the way you did the first layer, first framing the edge with cards.

4. Then put on the herringbone roof, leaving an opening again to line up the third layer.

You're almost ready for ritual sacrifices to the Mayan gods. Just put on three more layers, each smaller than the last.

    1. Line up the first cell of the next grid with the cards you left visible through the roof opening.

2. Add cells until you get a grid one card narrower than the one below, making a third story that should be just four cards square. Since this grid has a smaller "footprint," it should take just a few cards to frame the edge.

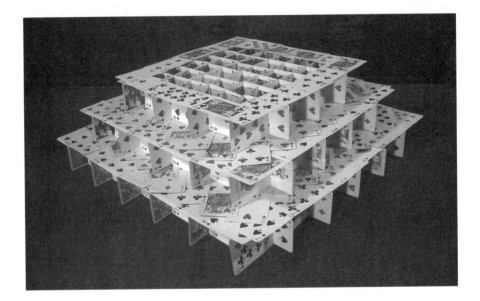

3. Lay a herringbone roof over the rest of the grid. Leave another hole and line up the next layer. It'll be just three cards square.

4. Put on the roof deck: Frame the grid and lay cards in a herringbone. Leave a hole again to line up the fifth and final story.

5. The last grid will be just two cards square. Line it up with the corresponding cards below.

6. Add a roof of four cards laid across the cells—one pair in one direction and the other pair in the other direction. Lean two vertical cards on each side for a final touch.

Of course, Mayan pyramids also have steps on at least one side. Here's how to make those:

1. Lean two cards against the first layer.

2. Lean two more cards against the second grid, tucking their bottom edges behind the cards leaned against the first layer. Do the same to create "stairs" on the third and fourth layers. Each "flight" will be held in place by the edge of the flight leading up to it.

For a final touch, you could put steeples on either side of the staircase. Hold three cards upright so two lean against a middle card. Adjust them until they balance.

There you go—a Mayan pyramid. And you didn't have to worry about drinking the water.

A Slab in the Face

This slab building is more difficult than it looks. Slabs require you to be more neurotic about roof decks and grid alignment. The taller you aim to build, the more obsessive you should be. If you're not ready for this, try it later.

You needn't follow these directions precisely. Your slab could be longer or shorter or taller, but to be a slab it shouldn't be more than a couple of cards wide. The slab I built here took me about an hour and used about five decks.

1. Start with the seed of all buildings: a single cell. Then add cards in one direction to create a row. If you make your row four and a half cards long, the way I have, you'll have seven boxes lined up.

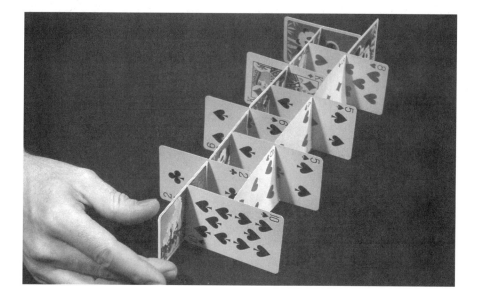

2. Lay two parallel rows of cards on top of the edges of the grid to make a roof. Overlap the cards slightly on their short sides. If one looks precarious, overlap its end with another card to tack it down. But don't overlap the two lines. They're like a divided highway with lanes that never cross, leaving a gap down the middle. This arrangement will make the roof look inadequate, but it'll all get tied together as you build.

Line up the first card of the second grid with the card below it. You should see it peeking out the edge, under the roof.

3. Set up cards to get another row of cells, with seven boxes lined up.

Roof this layer the way you did the first, with parallel rows of cards and a gap down the middle.

4. Line up your third layer the way you did the second. Every layer you add actually cuts the risk the structure will collapse. The weight of the cards pushes down on the ones below them and holds them in place.

Keep adding layers as high as you care to go. I stopped at eight. The more you add, the more likely cards near the bottom will flex and distort from the weight.

When you're done, see how many cards you can take out of the lower stories before the building collapses. Dissecting your building will give you confidence. You'll see how over-constructed even a simple building can be. This one stood even after I removed the centers of four floors.

A Shrine to Perseverance

- Japanese shrine
- Tokyo, 1995
- 250 decks
- 40 hours

I still regard this copy of a Japanese shrine, built for a television game show, as one of my best buildings. It had features I either hadn't mastered or hadn't attempted, including an overhang and a roof with an S curve.

I'm especially proud of this shrine because it was built under extreme conditions. First, I had to build all those tricky features on a larger scale than I'd planned—the ornamental wood base for the card shrine was about four feet square instead of the three feet I'd specified. I also had to move the unfinished shrine four times because the network needed the studio for other shows. Each time, I put a piece of plywood on top of the completed portion, stacked it with packs of cards to hold it in place, then held on to the platform to slow down the men who carried it about a thousand feet each way.

After that, it was no sweat handling a minor earthquake. Paul Shao, an Iowa State University architecture professor who came along on the trip, helped repair the damage—although I nervously begged him to stop. He may be the only reason I survived.

The television show was kind of a cross between *Hollywood Squares* and *Ripley's Believe It or Not*. Japanese celebrities guessed how I had built the shrine, how many cards I'd used, and other details. The demolition—when I pushed a man through the shrine—wasn't taped because it was considered sacrilegious.

The ornamental wood base holding the shrine is a copy of the one used to carry the real thing during an annual festival. I was told that the god honored by the shrine is believed to bring a good fish catch. The show's producers insisted I help carry an actual shrine in a festival parade. There I was, an Iowa farm kid, dressed in a loincloth and thin slippers and lugging a monument to good fishing.

It was a trip I'll never forget. Many of the fishing families who hosted me were very poor, yet they welcomed me into their homes and shared what they had.

Stackin' Alive

If you've stuck with card stacking this far, you've learned the basics. This chapter will add to and refine those tools, and show you more intricate ways to use them. In other words, you've learned the instrument; now it's time for your first symphony.

The Roar of the Cards

I built my first stadium when a trading-card company hired me to make a model of ALLTEL Stadium in Florida. The idea of building a stadium made of cards really took hold sometime later, when I built my first card city in St. Paul, Minnesota. There hadn't been space for a full-blown stadium, so I surprised myself by building a tight, bowl-shaped structure instead.

Stadiums or amphitheaters are merely layers of grids that follow a curve. The "spectators" are laid over the curved grids to create a bowl-shaped structure. Grids inside stadiums and domes are never normal. They're trouble. They're constantly in need of prodding and sculpting to make them fit. The following plans will show you how.

Remember: Your structures needn't look just like the illustrations. Don't be afraid to wing it. As you build, you might save the aces of spades or the face cards, and then put them in the stadium's "stands" so they look like a set of black spoons or a royalty convention.

Here's a simple amphitheater to start. It took me around two hours and used about seven decks.

Lay out cards in a **C** shape as a template for the stadium bowl. Start the grid so you can build along the back of the template but not on it, then build away from the template.

Build along the template's outer edges. Angle or omit grid cards any time they might encroach on the template. Notice how the six of diamonds on the right is angled slightly to make room for the arc.

Roof the edges. The cards laid along the curved edge should follow the template. Cover the rest with a herringbone, but leave a couple of holes to align the next grid. Don't fret if it doesn't line up exactly; just make the best of it. Since the first

layer doesn't have a fence, you also can align the second grid with cards visible on the edge of the first layer.

Build along the back of the structure first. Then build the rest of the grid to fol-

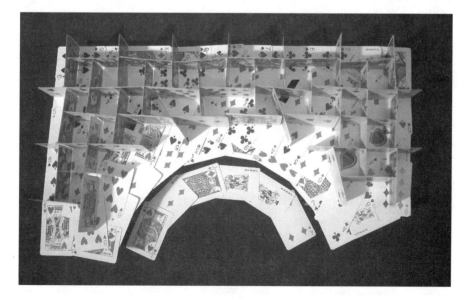

low the template, leaving a space of about half a card's length around the curved edge. Angle cards or omit them if they might intrude on that space.

Roof the edges, with cards following the template on the curved side. Put a herringbone across the rest of the grid and leave one or two holes for reference points.

Now add more roof cards—what I call a reacher course—along the curved edge. The first roof cards pinned down the edge and gave an idea of its shape; the reacher course extends the edge, making the second row of stadium "seats" stand up straighter when they're leaned against it.

Add a second layer of cards along the curved edge, making them hang over the edge a bit more than the first layer. Make sure they follow the template's shape.

Lay cards, spaced a half inch to an inch apart, along the back edge of the reacher course to tack it down. Finally, put another layer of cards on the rest of the grid's edge. This step is not essential, but it helps even out the roof surface. Cover the rest with cards in a herringbone pattern.

Move on to the third layer, and build it closer to the curved edge, tightening

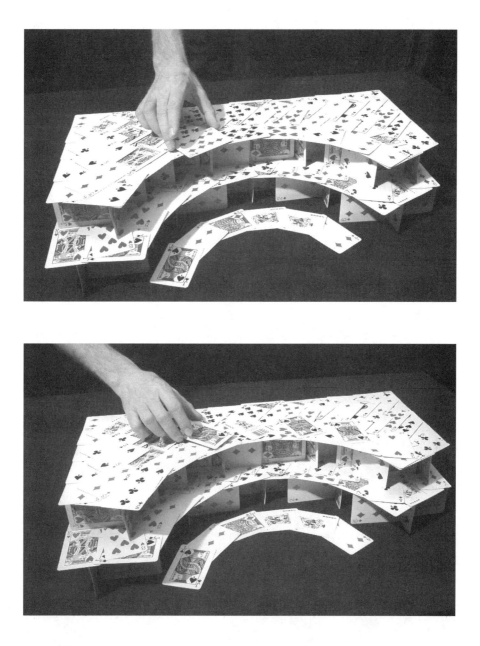

the arc so the cards it supports will stand up even straighter. I built around only one end of the arc, so the third row of seats will be shorter than the first two. This shape is just for looks; you can fill both sides of the arc if you wish.

Align the third grid at one of the roof holes or with the edge of the second grid. Build along the back of the grid, then fill in around the side. Once again, angle or omit cards that may encroach on the area around the curved roof edge. Leave a space of about half a card's length along the curve.

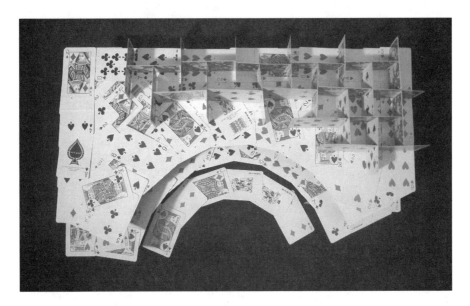

Put roof cards over the edges, including the curved edge. Put a herringbone over the rest of the grid.

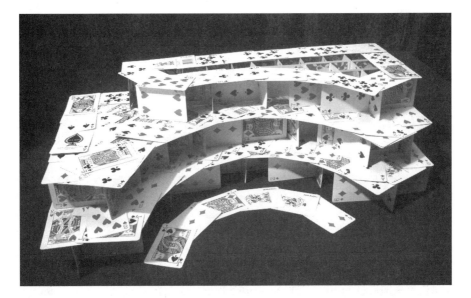

Add a reacher course to the curve. It needn't hang over far if the grid was built closer to the edge, but you still must be a bit of an artist and planner to make the grid support it. Think about where you want the cards to go, then find ways to put them there. In some cases, that may mean tucking a card into the grid to support the roof. Tack down the reacher course with widely spaced cards laid over its inside edge. Add more cards around the straight edges to even out the roof, and cover what little is left with a herringbone.

The final layer is another partial grid. Start at one end and follow the curve, angling or omitting cards as needed.

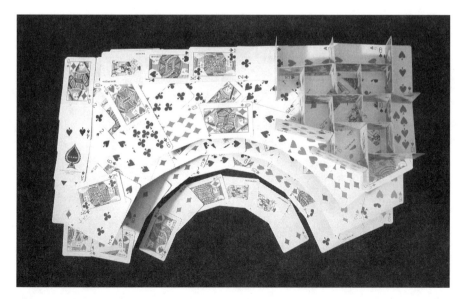

Then roof the grid, making the cards follow the curve again. You needn't worry about the roof being uneven unless you plan to build something on top of it, so use as many cards as you think are necessary. More usually is better, because the weight holds the structure in place.

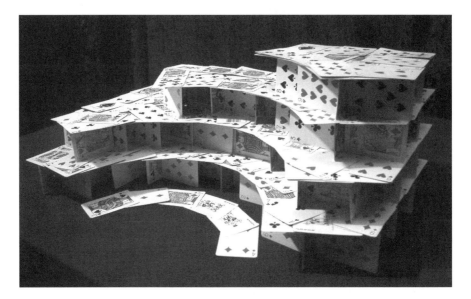

All you need now are "occupants" for the seats. Getting them to stand at the correct angle can be difficult, so don't get frustrated. Start at the bottom and take your time. Lean the lower ranks at a flatter angle. The upper rows will stand up

straighter. As you work your way up, some cards may fall and land behind ones in a row below. Just leave them if they're not visible.

Remove the template and lean cards against the edge of the first layer. I sometimes tuck each new card on the bottom row under the edge of the previous card.

Move on to the upper rows, and lean cards in against the curved grid edges. Each layer will help keep the row above it in place. Cards in the upper rows should stand up straighter than the ones below, creating a pleasing, cone-shaped effect.

That's a basic amphitheater. It's nothing fancy, but the bowl shape is impressive because it's unexpected. It shows how short, straight lines can work together to look like a single curved line.

Stand Up Straight

If building horizontal cells isn't challenging enough for you, try pipe columns and vertical walls. These shapes put the cards on their ends to make tall, thin structures. They'll test your patience because the cards are more likely to scoot around, but they're useful for a variety of buildings and ornaments.

Try a pipe column first.

1. Start with one card laid atop another at a right angle. This is a template for placing the upright cards. It also helps eliminate problems with the surface, especially when the column goes on another structure, and it makes

the column look neater. If your work surface is fairly smooth and flat, it might be easier to skip the template. Stand the first card at the edge of the area where the template cards overlap. Hold it loosely.

2. Lean the next card so it touches the first card a quarter inch to a half inch from its edge. Try to keep the tails to a minimum to make a leaner, fitter, and stronger column.

3. Keeping a loose grip on the first card, lean the third card in against the second.

4. Put the fourth card in place and lean the first card against it.

5. A four-card roof will help the column's stability—but it could still fall. Alternate the overlapping cards at right angles.

Columns are tricky because the cards touch near their edges rather than at their middles, where they're easier to balance. Yet these cards are stronger than they would be if they crossed at their middles. In this setup, the entire card supports weight atop the column. If the cards touched at their middles, only half of each card would lend support. Grids are stronger when cards cross at their middles because they're part of a larger system.

Take time to practice pipe columns. Try bridging them with cards. You'll develop an intuition about where to place the cards and how to hold them.

Now string columns together to make a vertical wall. A wall should be easier than a column, because the cards are in a system and their tails are longer. But walls are still difficult, so don't be disappointed if you don't get it immediately.

1. Lay cards side by side and overlap them slightly. Make the line as long as you want your wall to be. I've used eight cards. Then just build a pipe column: Put the first upright card on the end of the row and hold it loosely. Don't let go until the fourth card is set. Place the second card across the end of the first, setting it about a half inch from the second card's edge.

2. Card 3 goes across card 2, about a half inch in from the edge of card 3.

3. Card 4 goes across the end of card 3. Then lean the first card against card 4. Now just continue the wall down the row of cards you laid out. Put a fifth card across the tail that points down the row.

4. Put card 6 across the end of card 5. Its end will also brace the card next to it.

5. You've built two large cells. Now keep going.

6. As you build upright cells on the cards, see if you can "edit" them—tightening the angles at which they lean so they're more upright. Nudge them gently so they stand nearly straight up.

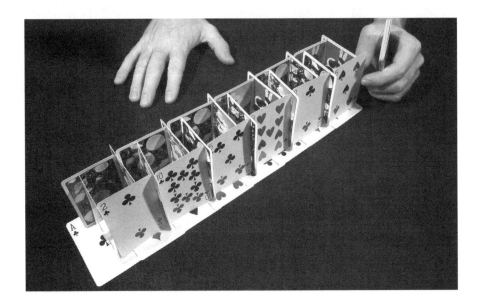

7. Notice the gap next to the last card on the wall.

A small nudge makes it disappear and pushes the card next to it so it's upright.

8. The roof is just two layers of lengthwise cards. They'll help keep the wall in place.

I added a steeple as a final touch.

You could stop now and see what weight this wall would bear—or you could go for a second story. There were only 40 cards in this wall, but it supported 101

decks—that's 5,454 cards, or a weight almost equal to another 136 layers built the same way. Cards in the bottom story bent—one even looked like an S—but none of them failed.

All the cards bent inward, where they were braced. The wall collapsed only after I removed some cards.

Back to the Bowls

This next stadium will stretch your skills a bit more than the first. In skiing terms, the first stadium gets a green diamond, meaning it's slightly difficult. This next stadium rates a black diamond, and the last gets a triple or quadruple black diamond—for experts only.

This stadium seems intimidating, but it's not really harder than the first—just bigger. Once again, your structure doesn't have to follow the illustrations exactly. You might skip some steps or alter the grids to make them follow the template. This one took me about three hours and used around twenty-three decks.

1. Start again with a curved card template. Put the first row of cells where you can complete it while just touching the arc, then add to it along the back.

2. The bigger the grid, the more room you'll have for the setbacks that support the seats, so add a couple of rows to the edges. Build the grid forward and along the sides to surround the arc without crossing it. If needed, nudge in the curved template and angle the cards for a good fit. I left a couple of members out of the back corners to create cutouts, but you can simplify the project by completing them.

As you might have already noticed, I trimmed the baseline on this stadium. Doing this is not necessary. Those cards do nothing to make the stadium stronger; they just make it look neater. To trim the baseline, just lay cards flat between the tails. Take care not to push them so close they cause a collapse. You may need to remove or gently pick up cards to make the baseline cards fit, especially on corners with cutouts. You also may need to slide the baseline cards carefully under the grid cards.

3. Fence the grid by leaning cards against the tails, then adding cards to close the gaps. Don't fence the curved edge. Edge the top of the grid with

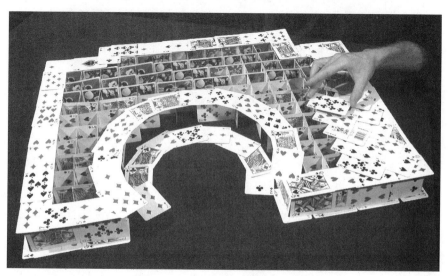

lengthwise cards; be sure they follow the template on the curved edge. Put on a herringbone roof, and leave two or three holes to line up the next grid.

4. Align the second layer over one of the roof holes. Start it along the back edge, then move in toward the arc. Omit cards or set cards at an angle as needed to follow the arc and leave a band of space about the width of a card around it.

Remember, you can put on the fence and roof as you build the grid. They'll help stabilize the structure if it's shaky. You also can slide cards in or out of the

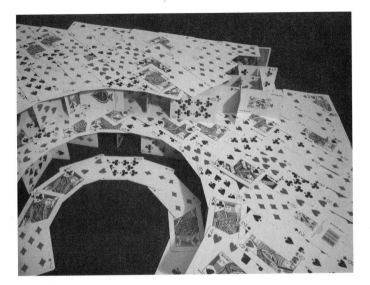

grid to make the fence stand up consistently. I made this grid shorter on the left end, but you could build it all the way to the edge.

5. Roof the second story by laying cards along the edges, then covering the rest of the grid with a herringbone, except for a couple of holes.

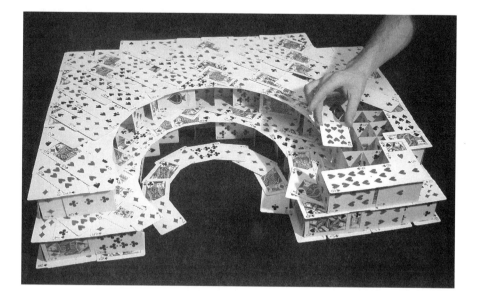

Now add a reacher course to the curved edge.

1. Lay lengthwise cards along the curve so they hang a bit over the edge.

2. Tack those cards down by overlapping their back edges with more cards spaced a half inch to an inch apart, then add more lengthwise cards along the straight edges. Without them, the curved edge would be thicker than the rest of the roof.

3. Line up the third tier of the stadium with the second. If needed, build an offset grid, as shown in Chapter 2, to fit the sides of the arc.

4. Put a fence on the grid, then edge it with cards and cover the rest with a herringbone roof. Don't worry about leaving holes this time; by now the grids are so small they don't need to line up. Add a reacher course along the curve, extending the roof edge and making it follow the template more tightly. Tack it down with widely spaced cards as before, and add more cards along the straight edges to make the roof relatively level.

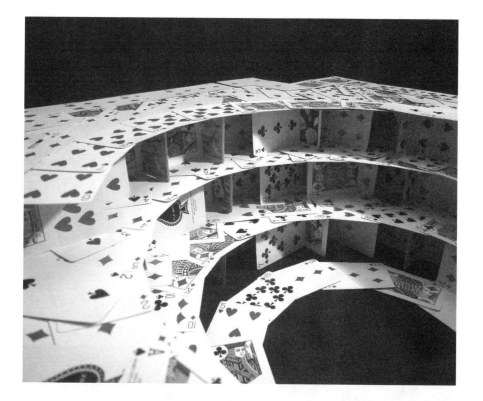

If you cut out the corners of the lower grids, you'll have to make the fourth layer an offset grid to fit the ends of the curve. If you didn't cut the corners, there should be space for a standard grid. This is an example of how the decisions made early in a project have consequences. Working my way out of such corners has forced me to develop new techniques.

An offset grid has one benefit: It won't need a fence because it looks neat without one.

1. Start the grid with a cell on one "arm" of the stadium's curve. Make it wide enough to approach the edge of the arc. Add more wide-set cells to extend the grid to the back edge.

2. Quickly lay overlapping cards across the grid. The sooner it's roofed, the less chance there is the grid will fall. Then build another wide-set grid along the

back, or widest side, and roof it. I didn't extend this grid completely around the curve, so the third row of seats won't go all the way around the stadium.

3. Now link the two grids with a roof. But first, to support the roof, insert cards where the grids meet.

4. Lay cards to follow the curve at the front of the grid and tack them down with widely spaced cards.

5. Now extend that curve and make it tighter with a reacher course. Tack it down with more cards.

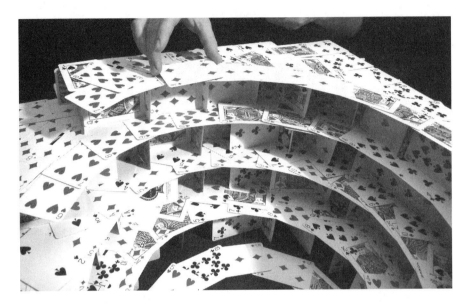

There's no shame in stopping here, but for extra credit, add a gallery—pipe columns supporting a cantilevered roof. Cross two cards at right angles for each of six columns, then move them around until they're evenly spaced—about a card's width apart, so they can be easily bridged. Build columns atop the crossed cards and hold them in place with roofs of four cards crossed at right angles.

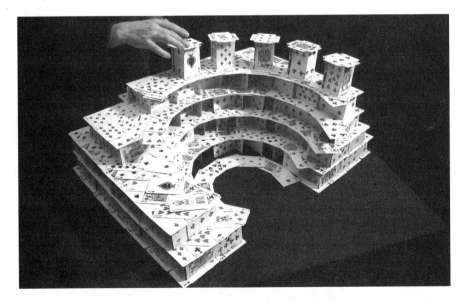

Now put on the overhanging roof. Galleries like this one aren't a science, and no two are the same. The key thing is to balance cards that hang out in space with extra cards along their back edges.

1. Bridge the columns with cards laid lengthwise so they line up with the back edges of the crossed roof cards. Put on a second layer to cover the ends of the first cards and tack them down.

2. Lay cards across the bridge so they extend over the front edge.

3. Tack those down with cards laid lengthwise over their back edges.

4. Add a final set of cards hanging farther over the front edge.

All that's left now is to fill in the stadium's seats.

1. Start with the bottom layer and lean cards against the curved grid edge. Nudge and scoot them into position as needed.

2. Move to the upper rows, where the grid follows the arc more tightly and the ledges are narrower. That should make the cards stand up straighter so they're easier to put in place.

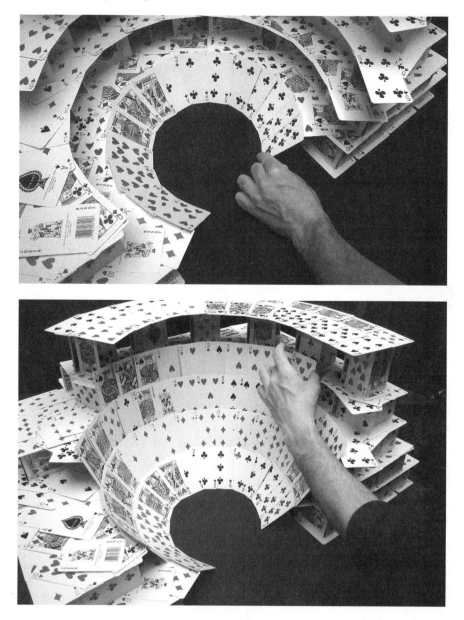

All you need now are guys selling peanuts and frosty malts.

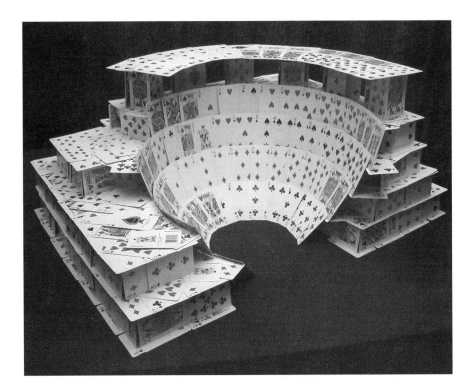

Super Bowl

This final stadium is almost off the scale for difficulty. I built it largely to show what's possible with the skills you've learned. The photos and instructions greatly condense the steps used to assemble this behemoth. Read them over to pick up some tips, but if you want to actually build the project, you'll need six to seven hours, about eighty-five decks, and a bachelor's degree in architecture.*

I created cutouts in the first grid by eliminating a card from each of the back

---

*Just kidding.

corners. One cutout was horizontal and the other vertical because the grid was ten and a half cards wide instead of a whole number, like ten or eleven.

The second layer was one course of cards smaller, leaving space around the edges. That gave the structure more ground presence, as if to spread out the

weight in a kind of bell shape. It would look odd without that—like a person without feet.

I put eighteen two-story columns and two vertical walls on top of the roofed second grid to support the third layer, then temporarily weighted them with whole decks to keep them in place. If you try something like this, be sure to build every column carefully. A single bad one could jeopardize the whole thing.

I used three cards in each column wall for added rigidity. Building in duplicate or triplicate is easiest if the cards are new and all the cards in each cell wall come from the same deck. When you use multiples, it's important to lay out the cards in advance, because once you start you won't have both hands available to deal them from the deck. Put the four stacks of cards within easy reach before beginning a cell.

Remember this, too: Well-built pipe columns made from single cards will be better and stronger than badly built columns made with triple cards.

I also flexed the column cards briefly to prestress them. Prestressing is necessary only when the cards will come under big loads. It "teaches" them to bend in a single direction when weight is applied. If you try this, don't flex too hard; you're not really bending them. Give the cards a quick squeeze with less force than if you were shuffling them. Be sure to flex them toward the side that will be braced. I always build with the card faces out, so I flex them with the backs out. When you finish, you shouldn't even be able to tell that you did it.

The concrete-and-steel beams in bridges and buildings often are prestressed for added strength, too. They're bent in the direction opposing the load they'll bear—if the weight will come down on the beam, it's prestressed so it curves slightly upward. Then the beam flattens when a load is applied.

Columns should be placed where they look attractive and can be bridged. Keep in mind that the farther apart they are, the more weight each will have to bear. They're subject to the architectural and engineering principle of point loading, in which weight is concentrated on small areas instead of distributed, as it is over a grid. Each column supports a tributary area, and all the weight in that area trickles down to the spot above the column. If the column isn't there, the structure won't work. You can see the same principle at work the next time you're in a parking garage under a building. Each of the huge columns regularly spaced through the garage supports a tributary area.

Next, after building the columns, I bridged them and filled in the spaces with a web of cards to make a solid floor. First I laid cards over the gaps between adjoining columns. I overlapped the ends of those cards with more cards to tack them down. I laid cards over the bridges to reinforce the floor's edges, starting with the curved edge.

Following this, I put on what I call a woven roof to cover the space separating the bridges and columns. In a woven roof, cards leave a minimal gap for each successive card. Cards are placed so they hang over the gap by a quarter or half length. The previous cards support each new card. I added cards to span the gaps, tacking down their ends with more cards as I went along. When finished, the roof was a solid mass of cards knit together. Their own weight helped hold them in place. Roofs like this won't support point loads, but a distributed load will be fine, so build grids on them, not pipe columns.

I don't really know where to begin a grid on a woven roof. I just start in a corner and hope for the best. I'm more careful about how I put cards in place when I build

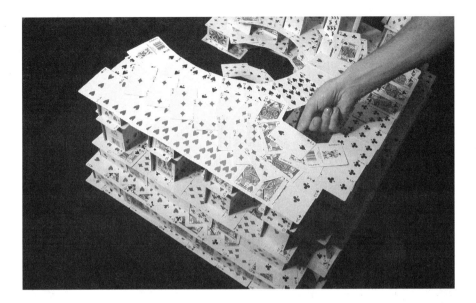

on such a surface. If I slide them into position, I could move the underlying cards and cause the grid to fall.

I used three-card thicknesses in this grid, not for strength but for weight to pin down the roof. The next grid was set a half-card in from the edge. I also inserted cards to extend the curved side so it would support the roof.

Moving the grid a half-card in left just enough space on the roof to support an

offset grid along the right side. It barely touched another offset grid I built along the back. I didn't finish the grid on the left side, so the row of seats was shorter.

The fourth layer was similar to the last—made with widely spaced cells. I built it close to the curved edge because the upper rows of cards stand more upright and require less space. Then I added a gallery similar to the one on the last stadium, except that this one has two-story pipe columns supporting it.

I put single-story pipe columns with a cantilevered roof on top of the first gallery. Once again I bridged the columns, then added cards to extend the front

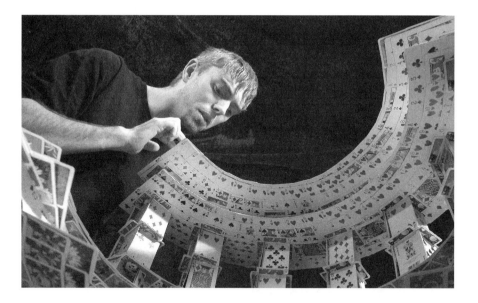

edge. When I was done, the roof edge extended more than a full card length into space.

The balcony seats were a big problem. The first row fell down many times because the cards couldn't get good traction. I scooted them around, adjusted the underlying cards, and kept trying. The upper rows went more quickly because those cards stood more upright and had the cards on the lower levels to brace them.

I was pleased with this project, even though I'd had my doubts about halfway through. The thing was getting so big I feared that the conical stadium section would get lost.

I sicced J.R. the cat on this building. It was kind of like "Attack of the Fifty-Foot Kitty" at the Super Bowl. He knocked most of the cards out of a couple of pipe columns, but they didn't fall.

After J.R. had his way, I stacked part of the gallery with books—*Structural Analysis* and *Load and Resistance Factor Design,* volumes 1 and 2, appropriately

enough. These pictures clearly show where the gallery failed. The blurry cards under the third column from the left were the first to go.

Capitol Idea

- Iowa Capitol
- Des Moines, Iowa, August 2000
- 2,000 decks
- 11 days

Though the Iowa State Fair paid me, I built the Iowa Capitol in cards as much for myself as for them. I thought about the project for months, but exactly how I would do it was kind of a mystery—and that's what I liked. It stretched me.

The Capitol was really like eighteen or twenty separate buildings standing within a micron of one another and collectively casting the image of one building. Because of the size, I had to complete some pieces before others could be done—and do them with great precision. If a building was one-sixteenth of an inch lower than the one next to it, they couldn't be joined. That meant the columns supporting the dome, for instance, had to be nearly identical. I spent days making sure they were.

The size also meant I couldn't build the Capitol of solid card cells. That would have taken at least twice as long—and it wouldn't have looked as cool. Instead, it was mostly hollow, like a warehouse, with perimeter walls and pillars. When I finished, it was more open space than standard grid pattern.

The main dome was massive—in hindsight, more massive than necessary. It was built like a bunker when a chicken coop would have sufficed. I'd never built a dome that big, and it sat on a dozen precarious columns six feet in the air. I also hadn't built pipe columns destined to hold so much weight for such a long time. Each was essential for success.

The columns on the front portico, one of the building's more recognizable features, determined the scale of the whole project because they had to be in proper proportion. It also was a challenge to make them attractive. Columns will always look a bit cartoonish because I never bend cards and my basic structures are squares. I had to find a balance between cartoon and lifelike. The low, sloped roofs

also threw me. I came up with a solution—a combination of grids with cards inserted into them—just as I needed it.

I worked in the cultural center, among paintings, sculpture, and other visual displays. That made my project more like art than performance, but I also had to work without air-conditioning in the heat and humidity of an Iowa August. The only things I used more than cards were water and Kool-Aid. I had gallon jugs all around, and I heard several spectators claim they held glue. I usually responded by grabbing one and taking a long drink.

When I knocked down the Capitol, I could tell it was overbuilt—like most of my projects. And it would have been more successful if I'd made it 15 to 20 percent larger, so I could explore the building's details more. But that was impossible in the time I had. The ability to experiment with detail is why I want to build something else huge—with lots of time and a good work space.

A Stack Above the Rest

Many of my buildings weren't instantly cool. They got that way with generous adornment. Adornment transforms simple waffles into amazing structures. Unusual roofs are part of that.

In this chapter, you'll see how structures can be creatively "shingled" to mold them into unexpected shapes. Instead of boxes or bowls, you'll see buildings with steep roofs, curved roofs, and domes.

Let Us Pray

If you put stairs on the Mayan pyramid or seats in a stadium, you've already done what's needed for a pitched roof. All the work is in setting up ledges to support the shingles. Installing the shingles can be difficult, but it's just finish work, so take it easy and be patient. Difficult things often are the most cool.

To demonstrate, here's a simple structure I turned into a church. The directions are condensed, but the building is simply made of grid layers, each one narrower than the one below it. Beware, though: This is a wolf in sheep's clothing. It took several tries to put on the shingles, but if you can do this one, you can master most roofs. It took me about two difficult hours and used eleven decks. I saved the aces of spades for shingles.

Start with a basic, rectangular grid. I built mine three cards wide by five cards long. I fenced it and put on a herringbone roof.

Center each successive layer over the one below. To center a grid, build one row along the back edge, then shift it left or right as you learned in Chapter 2 until it looks centered. Try to stick with that line as you finish the grid. Fence just the ends; the sides will be covered with shingles. Edge the grid with lengthwise cards, and cover the rest with a herringbone.

Each layer should be narrower by a consistent amount—a card or half-card length. You may have to offset a grid slightly to get it right. Make the roofs of each level simple: a line of cards along each edge and a single herringbone down the middle. During construction or just before shingling, adjust the roof edges of each level or add cards to them so the shingles will have a consistent slope.

Lay shingles on the bottom row first. Overlap the cards, and nudge their bottom edges into position as necessary. The second and third rows will be more difficult, but don't bother rescuing a card if it falls behind a row below it. If a lot of cards fall, check to see if the edge they're leaning on is out of line or has protruding cards.

The ridge will be hairy. It's a series of steeples, and if they're not balanced right when they're released, they'll fall and knock down cards below them. If it

gets frustrating, try putting the steeples on first, then adding the shingles. Remember, a steeple has three cards: one in the middle with one leaned against each side. (I used three cards on each side against two cards in the middle. The added weight made it easier to stand them up.) Assemble each steeple on your work surface just as it will be on the building. Then grab it between your thumb

and index finger and hoist it into position. Hang on to the cards and adjust them until they balance.

You can stop there, or add a bell tower of wide-set cells. I used three-card thicknesses and fresh cards for stability. Each cell was topped with four cards, two laid side by side topped with two side by side at right angles to the first two. I laid six cards atop the last wide-set cell and topped that with a pipe column made with three-card thicknesses. The column had a roof of six cards set at right angles to each other. I put on another steeple for a properly sacred touch.

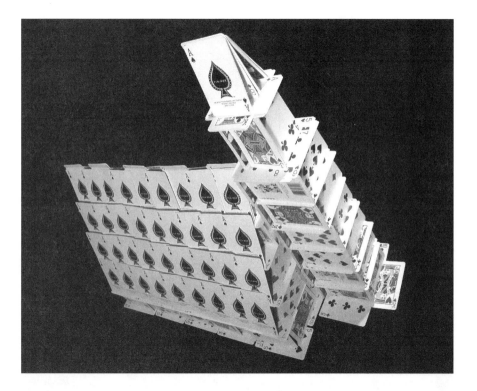

Your First Kiss

The next structure is a kind of squarish Hershey's Kiss. It has a domelike, curving roof with smooth corners. It took me ninety minutes and used seven decks, including two decks of aces of spades.

1. Start with a standard, four-card-square grid. Roof the edges with length-wise cards but omit the corner cards.

2. Cover the corners with single cards laid at an angle, and put a herring-bone over the rest of the grid, leaving a hole over the center intersection.

3. The second layer will be three and a half cards square. Build the first cell over the hole, but don't put the first cards right on it. Instead, center the first cell over the intersection. Build the rest of the grid carefully and there will be a ledge about a quarter of a card wide all the way around. If necessary, center the grid by shifting it as you learned in Chapter 2.

4. Roof this grid the same way you did the first, with lengthwise cards over all the edges except the corners. Cover those with single cards laid at an angle. Put a herringbone on the rest of the grid, but leave a hole over one intersection.

5. The third layer will be aligned with the second grid, so place the first two cards such that they're directly over the ones visible through the hole. It'll be two and a half cards square. The roof follows the same pattern: lengthwise cards on the edges except for the corners. Cover those with angled cards, and lay a herringbone on the rest. I added extra cards to the roof for ballast.

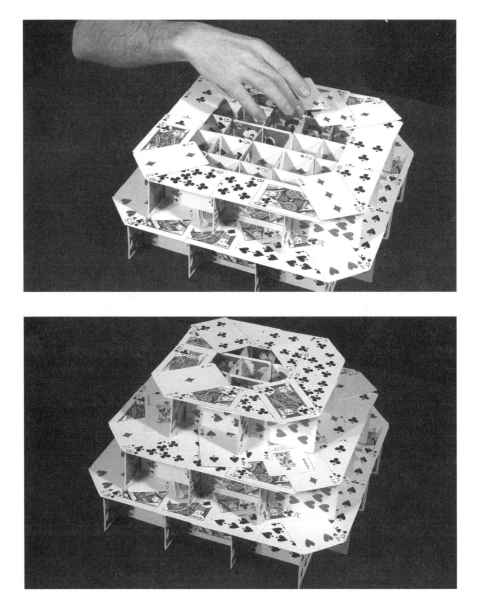

Now look it all over and pay attention to the edges. Carefully nudge the roof cards so everything is straight. The more they're aligned, the easier it will be to shingle the structure.

1. The fourth and last layer has just enough room for a wide-set cell. Roof it with ten or twelve cards, laid two abreast with each pair at a right angle to the previous pair.

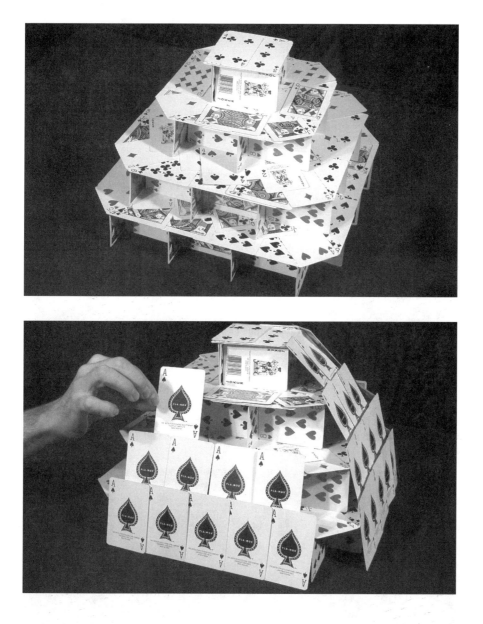

2. Now shingle the structure, starting at the bottom, where the cards will be completely upright against the grid's straight edges. The bottom row has five cards. The second one has four, and the third one up has three. The higher the row, the more horizontal the cards will lie—just the opposite of stadiums, where cards in the lower rows leaned at flat angles and cards in the higher rows were almost vertical. Lay two cards against each side of the wide-set cell.

3. Lean shingle cards against the angled edges. Do this carefully—sometimes the corner shingles will lie under the cards on either side; sometimes they'll be on top. If you knock shingles off the straight edges, try putting on the corners first.

4. Add a pipe column and top it with six cards laid at right angles. Lean a shingle against each side. I also installed an apron by laying lengthwise

cards around the structure. This is an entirely optional step, but it gave the building more of a presence at the base.

Getting Dome-esticated

If you succeeded with the last couple of projects, you're ready for a dome. Domes look impossible, but a second-grader can understand them: They're layer cakes, with each grid smaller than the one below. Cards lean against the grids to make the roof look curved. Each dome is different; you must understand how it works and invent a way to finish it. Domes require the most on-the-fly engineering of all card structures.

You'll see what I mean in this next project—a small dome that took me about ninety minutes and used about eight decks, including a deck of aces of spades for shingles.

1. Start with a standard four-card-square grid. Fence it, and lay on a standard herringbone roof with a hole over the center. Align the second grid with the first. Make it three cards square, but omit the corners.

2. Roof the edges of this grid with an octagon: Center a lengthwise card on each edge, then link them with angled cards.

3. Now lay eight cards across the octagon like spokes in a wheel. Line up their back edges with the octagon's inside edge.

4. Adjust the first layer of "spokes" so it's reasonably round, then lay more cards across the octagon until the edge is a nearly smooth circle.

5. Cover the remainder of the grid, but leave another hole over the center to align the next grid. Finally, add another layer of spokes to stabilize the edge.

6. Align the next grid, and build it two cards square. Lay a card lengthwise between the tails on each side for added stability. Then insert an upright card in the center.

7. Roof the grid with cards on both sides of the insert and lay lengthwise cards around the edges to form another rough-edged circle. Put on enough cards to minimize the sawteeth caused by their corners.

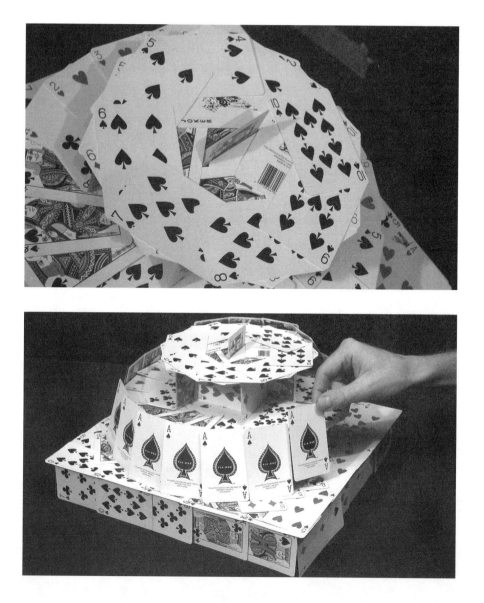

Now it's time to add shingles. They can be a headache, so remain calm. If you like, check the dome's slope by laying a row of shingles on one side. If the slope isn't right, adjust it by carefully pulling or pushing on the round edges.

1. Put the lowest row on first so they brace cards on the second layer. I tried this row with single cards, but they weren't heavy enough to brace the upper row, so I made each first-row shingle four cards thick. Three probably would have worked.

2. Say a little prayer as you do the second row. I like to build domes, but getting the shingles to stay in place can be frustrating. The biggest culprits are uneven edges behind the cards. If cards refuse to stand up, try adjusting the edge of the roof that supports them.

3. This next step—placing cards on the upright insert—looks impossible. To do it, lean a card against each end of the insert.

4. Those two shingles will support two crossed cards.

5. Lean shingles against each side of the crossed cards, and lay shingles over the two that support them.

6. Finally, put shingles over the gaps between those cards.

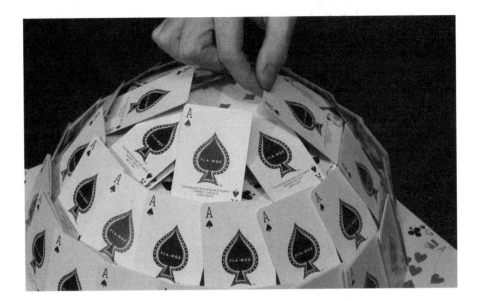

That's the dome. I added an apron and leaned cards against the bottom grid, but that's just for looks.

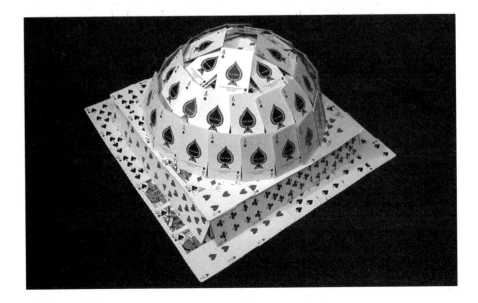

Your dome may not be as clean as this one. It takes practice to make the shingles stand up straight with the proper overlap.

Thunder Dome

Domes have been regarded as landmark engineering feats since the days of the Roman Empire. Famous ones like St. Peter's Basilica and the Pantheon in Italy were built without the advantages of modern equipment, such as cranes, or modern materials, such as steel. Everything in them is held together by gravity and compression—the weight of the pieces pushing on one another.

Big card domes actually can be easier to build than small ones because the large ones have more room, and the cards lie flatter at the top. This next dome, for example, sits on two grids and a ring to give it authority. With the base, it took me about four hours and used around thirty-one decks, including aces of spades laid on as shingles.

The first grid is seven cards square. Adjust it as you build, straightening out cards and nudging the interior ones so everything lines up. Fence it, and put on a standard roof with a hole over one grid intersection. Align the second grid, and make it six cards square.

Fence the grid, and put on another standard herringbone roof with edge cards. Edge the roof with a second layer of lengthwise cards, and align the third grid with the second. This grid will be five cards square, but you'll later remove cards to make it round.

1. Start a circle around the edges of the third grid by placing cards at the center of each straight edge, as at the points of a compass. Then lay cards at an angle between them to make an octagon. You can see in the photo

how the cards should be angled from the way they cut across cells in the grid below. See how it's starting to look like a circle?

2. Align more cards with the inside edges of the previous cards to flatten the angles gradually, and blend the cards into a rough-edged circle.

3. Place four lengthwise cards in a box over the grid's center intersection, then lay cards in a spiral around the hole. Edge the roof again with lengthwise cards that follow the circle.

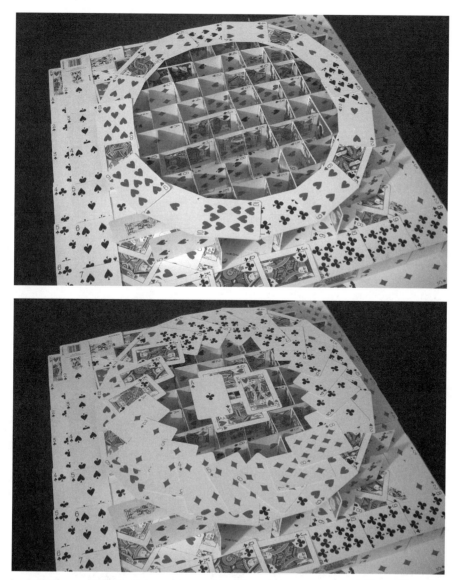

Now, carefully remove grid cards that protrude from under the round edge. They should come free without disturbing the grid, since the roof is holding it in place. Cards that barely stick out can be nudged so they're at an angle or gently pushed deeper into the grid.

1. Put on a fence. This may be the hardest step, because you'll have to make flat cards fit a round surface. Sometimes there will be something to hold the card in place; sometimes there won't.

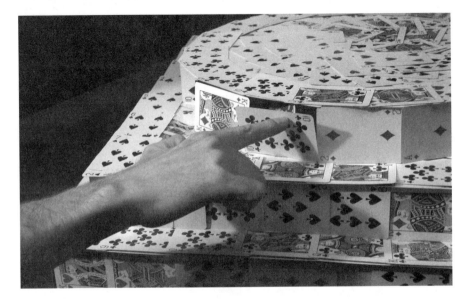

2. Lay a reacher course across the card circle, and align its back edge with the circle's inside edge. These cards will be the base for the first layer of shingles.

3. Tack down the reacher course with a spiral of cards over its back edge.

4. Align the next grid with the one below it, and build it so it nearly reaches the inside edge of the reacher course, giving it a roughly round shape. This

one worked out to be four cards across at its widest points. Start the round roof edge by laying cards on the centers of the grid's four sides. Place angled cards between them to make an octagon. Add more cards to cover the gaps,

and smooth the circle's edge so it follows the lower circle. Strive for perfect roundness, but don't worry too much. Then, remove or nudge in any grid cards protruding from under the roof.

Check how the shingles will lie against the grid's edge. The bottom row should be close to upright. If necessary, add a reacher course of cards laid across the circle.

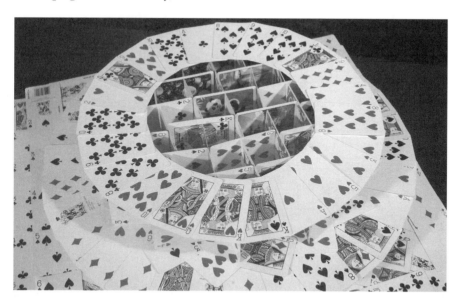

Finally, finish this level and prepare for the next by framing the grid's center with four roof cards, then spiral cards around the hole to cover the rest of the grid. It won't take many.

1. To give the fifth layer extra heft, I used triple cards because space was getting tight. It probably wasn't necessary. Align the grid over the roof hole and

build it out to a rough circle shape. It worked out to be three cards across at its widest points. It should be easy to figure out where to start the circular roof edge since the grid is so small. Lay a card on the center of each side, then make an octagon with angled cards between them.

2. Check the roof's shape again. You may have to add reacher courses or adjust the edges to get the right slopes.

3. Tack down reacher courses with cards overlapping their back ends, then add cards to cover the grid. By now, a hole over the grid's center is optional; space is so limited it no longer matters if the next layer is aligned.

It took several tries to get this last, tiny grid positioned to support the top shingles. To make it work, I added a third reacher course to extend the edge and tacked it down again in the center. That seemed easier than pulling and nudging to extend the previous reacher course.

1. The last grid is a single cell placed so it frames the circle's center. Lean cards against each tail, and place four upright cards so they stand around the center box. Cross the tails to finish the cells and brace the uprights.

2. Roof the grid by laying cards alongside the inserts, then perpendicular to them so cards hang over the edges on all four sides.

Turn that roof into a circle with lengthwise cards laid at angles. Put on several layers to smooth the circle's edge. It'll never be perfectly round, but try to minimize the protruding card corners. Finally, put four cards atop the inserts, each at a right angle to the previous one, and start shingling.

1. Put on the lowest row of shingles first, so they stand almost completely upright. I used three cards behind each ace for stability, but single cards may have worked just as well. Carefully shingle the second and third rows, overlapping the cards slightly. I used multiple cards on the second row.

2. The top row of shingles seemed to have too little pitch, so I extended the edge with another set of cards and leaned four cards on it. You may or may not need to move the roof edges in or out to make your shingles lean as you desire.

3. Cover the gaps between the four top shingles, and add a steeple if you like. I also put a circle of cards around the dome and an apron on the square base, then leaned cards against the bottom story.

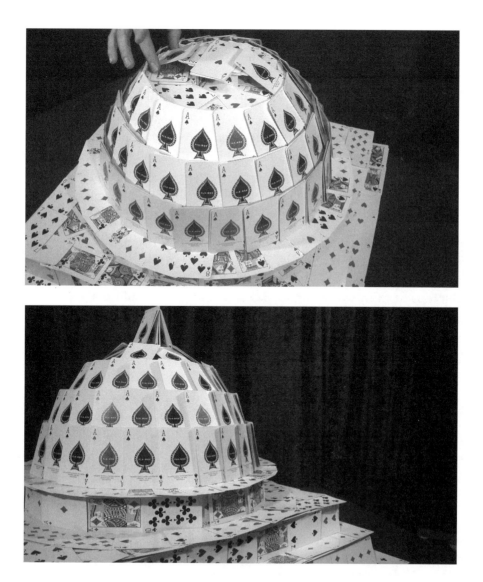

This is an impressive dome, but it isn't much more difficult than the previous one. It shows again what can be done when a few basic techniques are combined.

Home Run

- Ebbets Field model
- Cooperstown, New York, March 2001
- About 30,000 trading cards
- 50 hours

I'd built trading-card stadiums before, but the one I did to promote the baseball cards Post put in its cereals was unique because of the subject and location. The company wanted a stadium that would be more about baseball history and the national sense of the game than about any one team. They chose Ebbets Field, the vanished home of the Brooklyn Dodgers. The Baseball Hall of Fame was the natural place to build it.

The next problem was the cards. I was skeptical about building with actual baseball cards because they're usually too thick and glossy, but one of the two kinds Post planned to distribute worked fine. Topps actually made the cards, and the company was reluctant to print extras for me because doing so would make the cards less valuable, but in the end I had more than enough.

The size of the project made it tricky. There was no way I could reach parts of the stadium once I got started, so I had to assemble the work surface as I built the stadium. I built the C—the main grandstand—first, while standing in the "field," about where the pitcher's mound would be. Then I slid in another part of the work surface to build the field and, finally, the outfield fence.

Building something that no longer exists also was unusual. I had to examine pictures and make some educated guesses. It really wasn't a problem, because most of the people who looked at my work were comparing it against a photo, too. Just the fact that I built it and made it look anything at all like the real stadium impressed people.

The project was masterfully marketed. There were T-shirts, banners, and other materials. A TV crew followed me through the whole thing, then edited together a

story that was offered free via satellite to local stations. A media report later found that the piece aired on dozens of TV stations. Newspapers also ran photos available through wire services. Altogether, almost 10 million people read about the project or saw it on television.

The Baseball Hall of Fame people were wonderful and had everything perfectly arranged. Cooperstown is a nice upstate New York town, and the bed and breakfast where I stayed was excellent. The owners even brought cookies to me at the Hall of Fame.

Stack Me
to the Moon

Building towers requires a certain mind-set. You have to realize they're no harder than building grids. They're also like working in a factory: You do the same thing, over and over. Do it with consistency and conformity, and you'll build tall, straight towers. The hard part is maintaining that consistency despite the repetitive work.

You probably already know about consistency and uniformity if you've built one of the large structures found earlier in the book. But you have to be obsessive about these qualities to build good, strong towers. If you can't duplicate a pattern repeatedly, your towers could be crooked and unsteady, unable to reach astounding heights.

So if you've been a bit haphazard up to this point, get disciplined—and reach for the sky.

A Starter Stack

Tall is a relative term when it comes to card towers. A six-foot, box-shaped tower is tall for its type. A slab building like the one in Chapter 2 is tall for its shape, at three feet. The following building probably could go as high as six feet, but it looks impressive at just under three feet because it's thin. It's a good, basic tower that should take one to two hours and five and a half decks.

1. The lowly single cell is the heart of this tower. By now, putting four cards together in a box should be second nature to you. Fence it with cards leaned against each tail, followed by more cards to cover the gaps.

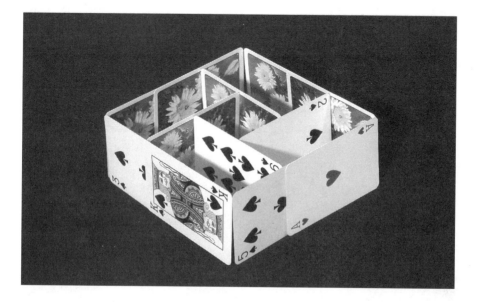

2. The roof is more important here than in most of the previous structures. In tall structures, small roof problems can mean big trouble if they're repeated. For this roof, lay four cards so they hang over the edges by about a quarter of an inch and do not overlap. If they overlap, the layers that go on the roof could be unstable.

3. Put on four more cards, moving in the opposite direction from the first four. The second set of cards should cover the gaps between the first ones and hang over the edge by about the same amount. Don't overlap them. The roof should be two cards thick everywhere.

Now follow the same steps for the second and third stories. Maintain the same pattern—using precisely twenty cards per layer—and you'll build a sturdy tower.

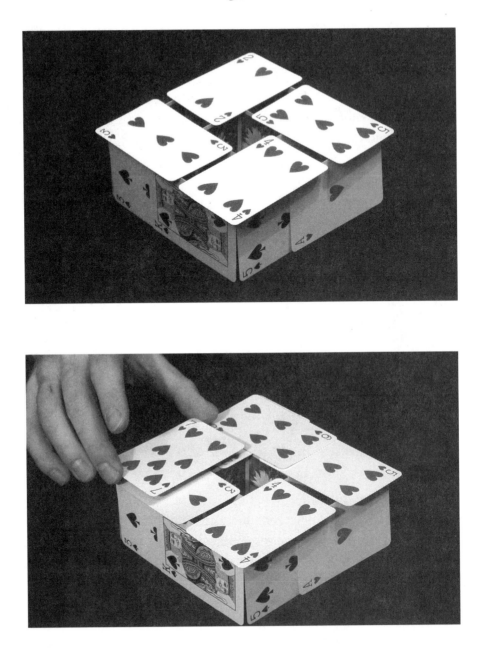

1. Put the first card on its edge about a quarter-inch out from the hollow square. The far end also should be about a quarter inch beyond the hole. Remember to let it float between your fingers, and finish the cell with three more cards around the roof hole. Each card should be

about a quarter-inch out from the hole. Fence the cell the way you did the first one.

2. Stick to the same pattern for the roof: four cards around the center hole and four more in the opposite direction. Don't overlap cards in the layers.

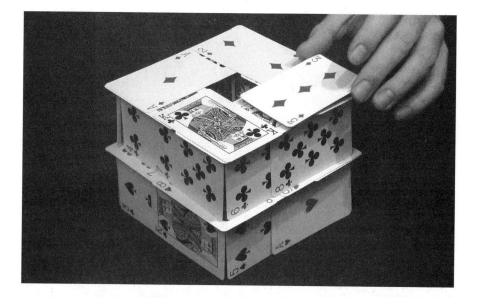

It would be too repetitive to show how the third, fourth, or fifth layers went on; they're the same as the first two. That's what makes this tower—and buildings in real life—tall and strong: repetitive geometry and mass. The more stories you build, the more stable it will be—to a point. Card towers that have the same dimensions all the way up can get top-heavy. That's why my tallest towers are all kind of stretched-out pyramids: wide at the base and gradually narrower toward the top. The big base makes the thin peak more stable.

I finally stopped building this tower with fourteen stories and topped it with a "penthouse" composed of a wide-set cell roofed with six cards.

I could easily have made this tower much taller. It supported a heavy book with no problems.

Practice building a few towers, including some based on broader grids—two, three, or four cards square—before tackling something really tall or difficult.

Plumb Crazy

Early in my career, I figured out the secret to tall card towers: keeping them as straight as possible. It began with my first record-setting structure in Spirit Lake, Iowa, when John Franklin, an engineer for whom I worked, suggested I use a plumb bob.

A plumb bob is a weight hung from the ceiling on a string. The weight keeps the string perfectly vertical, and as long as the tower follows that line it too will be straight. A plumb bob helps me ensure that the grids are aligned as I stack them. Towers with unaligned grids might lean because one side is more rigid than the other.

People who watch me work think the string supports the tower, but I'm actually careful to make sure that the string doesn't touch any part of it. If it did, the line would no longer be vertical and the entire tower could be crooked. The string just hangs down the center and stays there until the tower is finished, when I carefully pull it out. I use a plumb bob on all of my tall towers—which means they all have empty shafts through their centers.

A bob probably is unnecessary for those who consistently line up each new grid with the "crosshairs" of intersecting cards in the grid below. Those who are determined to build huge towers may want to use a plumb bob, but beware: It doesn't make things any easier or safer. The string could destroy a lot of stacking if it is bumped, especially in the early stages or on a relatively narrow tower. You must be more body conscious so you don't catch a finger or a thumb on the string and pull it through the building.

With those warnings in mind, here's how to use a plumb bob. First, tie a small weight with a string in a loose loop, so the object hangs straight down. Metal nuts,

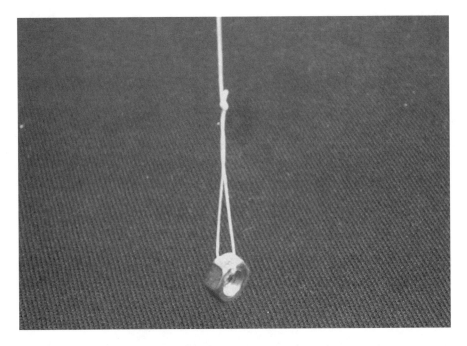

washers, or fishing sinkers work well. Attach the other end to the ceiling so the weight is in about the center of your building area.

Start the first grid with two cards placed so they meet about a quarter-inch from the bob.

Finish the cell with two more cards. The idea isn't to build so the string hangs down the *center* of the cell; that's hard to do consistently with every grid. The idea is to build an intersection that is nearly touching the string at or near the grid's center.

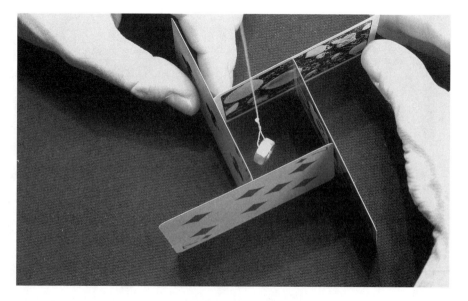

This method will work with any size grid. I built one just two cards square, then carefully roofed it so a hole was left around the string and over the intersection nearest to it. The roof used three cards abreast on each side, then six cards at right angles to the first six. Notice how the center cards are scooted out a bit to leave room around the string.

Start the second layer by lining up the first two cards with the string and the crosshairs visible through the roof hole.

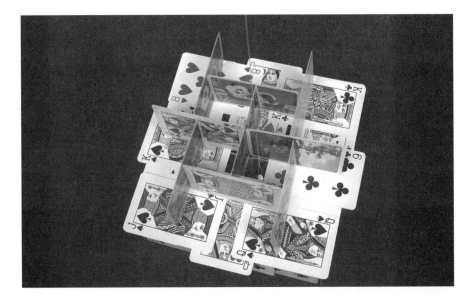

Remember to be careful. If your finger or thumb catches on the string, you'll pull the weight through the building.

I made just five stories, but in theory this building could go as high as seven feet if it was straight and tapered into a thin pyramid. I know this because of a guideline I discovered: A tower can have one foot of elevation for every inch of length on any one side of its base. Cards are about three and a half inches tall, so a grid two cards square is seven inches on a side and could thus grow into a seven-foot tower. A tower that is ten and a half inches by fourteen inches at the base could be ten to fourteen feet tall. The base of my last record-setting tower had eight cards on each side, for a total of twenty-eight inches. I made it a little over twenty-five feet tall, but in theory it could have been twenty-eight feet tall.

I figured this out over years of card stacking. When I've exceeded the formula's limit, the results have been risky—towers that were loose and without much backbone. Buildings that violate the rule seem top-heavy; when they're bumped, they sway slowly. That shows they're taking time to recover. Properly built towers are more rigid and recover faster. When they're bumped, they wiggle rather than sway.

As I've said, my highest towers usually resemble tall, thin pyramids because the grid gradually gets smaller as the structure grows. I usually don't stair-step them, making each layer smaller than the one before. I like to keep the grids bigger, because the added weight makes the tower stable. Nevertheless, there is a point when any tower will be less stable if I don't taper it.

Empire Builder

New York's Empire State Building held the title of world's tallest building for so long, it's often what people think of when the word *tall* comes up. So why not try to replicate it in cards? This tower used about forty-five decks and took me about four hours; your time could be longer, unless you've really mastered towers.

1. Start with a three-card-by-five-card grid. I used three cards in each member for added weight. Trim the baseline by laying cards between the tails, then fence it and add a standard roof, with a hole over the center intersection. Repeat for the second layer. The third layer will be three cards by four cards, with parts of the fence omitted to make a rectangular cutout in the center of each side.

2. Roof the grid carefully to avoid large overlaps, and leave a hole so the center intersection is visible. Leave the cutouts uncovered.

3. The fourth and fifth layers are the same as the third. Align each grid with the one below it. The sixth layer will be different. Align it with the fifth layer, but build it just three cards wide and two cards deep. Then add a card to each of the four tails that stick out toward the front and back corners (not

the ones in the center, where the cutouts are) so each is about a quarter-card longer. Lean cards against the center tails—the ones that point toward the cutouts.

4. Use fences to box each end of the grid. The fences will get rid of the cutouts on the ends, but keep the cutouts on the front and back. The fences will stay completely separate, with gaps next to each cutout.

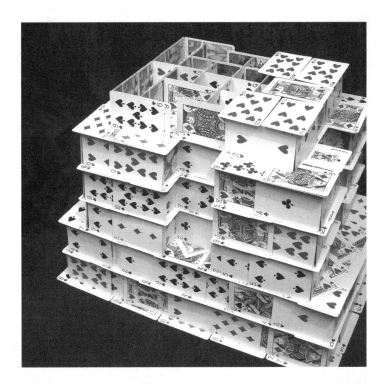

The "ears" on the grid will make it more difficult to roof, because some cards will have to be set in. Avoid making the roof more than two cards thick at any spot. As layers are added to a tall building, inconsistent overlaps can multiply to create uneven grids and leaning towers.

1. Lay cards across the grid, with two lengthwise on each corner and two across the middle.

2. Overlap those with cards in the opposite direction. The crosshairs at the grid's center should still be visible through a small crack.

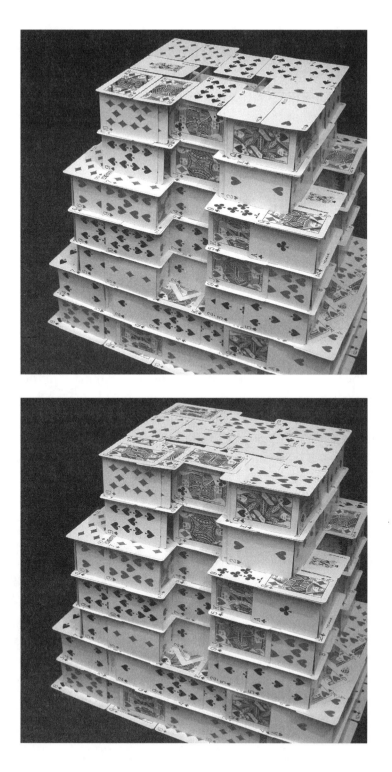

Now comes the monotonous part: building multiple layers the same way. As you go, be careful that the cards extending the front and back tails don't creep in. It's easy subconsciously to make them shorter with each layer until the cutout disappears and the roof cards don't fit. Force yourself to make them consistently stick out by a quarter-card.

You also should be careful not to subconsciously shift grids toward you as you build them. If you stay in the same place the whole time you build a tower, it could start leaning in that direction. Either change your position frequently or take care to ensure the grids don't creep in your direction.

Check over the tower every few layers. Small problems can become big ones if they aren't addressed early. For instance, I noticed that the roof on the left side of the grid had developed a slight upward bulge. Without repair, it could have led to a crowned surface that would have been almost impossible to build on. I put extra roof cards on the left corners in several layers until the arch was gone. I could even have made it sag slightly on that side—not a bad thing, since saging actually pushes the cards together. I kept monitoring that edge to see if the arch returned. If it had, I would have added cards in a few layers to correct it again.

The taller the tower, the more stable it should be. I bumped this one when it was thirteen stories tall, but it lost only a few easily replaced fence cards. I can tell how stable a tower is by the way it reacts to bumps and vibrations. A big tower, two or three feet square at the bottom and five or six feet tall, will shake only a little because it weighs about a hundred pounds. It has the shape and geometry—and a lot of the physics—of a refrigerator.

I used the same pattern through the twentieth layer, then created another setback, or slightly smaller layer. It took some experiments to get it right.

1. Build the first cell over the grid below it so the crosshairs of intersecting cards are in the center of the new cell's box. Make the cell so it's slightly rectangular, running from front to back. The cells on each side of the first also will be slightly rectangular, with the long part stretching across the grid, not front to back. When finished, the grid will be two and a half cards wide and one and one half cards deep at the middle. Then add cards to the two tails pointing to the front and back on each side so each is about a quarter-card longer. The extensions will make the grid two cards deep. Fence it much as you did the earlier layers, with independent boxes around each side and one card on the front and back to make the cutouts.

2. The roof isn't as critical because it will support only a few layers. Lay four cards across each end, overlapping them slightly, and four cards across those, one at each corner.

3. I put two more cards over the middle, parallel to the cutouts, and one at an angle over the center.

This may be the most difficult layout of any in the building, but at least it has to be built only two more times, for a total of three.

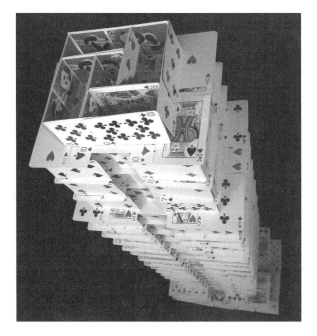

The twenty-fourth layer will be set back again so the cutouts disappear. It's a standard single cell, offset slightly to make the center box a rectangle with the length running from front to back. Fence it the way you would a regular cell.

The roof can be a bit different because it supports so little. Overlap three cards on each side, then put two cards across them on opposite corners.

The next floor will be the same—a single cell with a slightly elongated center. You may put the roof on twice to tack it down.

Now for the mooring mast—a dressed-up, three-story pipe column.

1. Lay two cards crossed at a right angle over the center of the grid, then stand four upright cards into a column, the way you learned in Chapter 3.

Once again, I used three cards in each member. Dress the column—an optional step that makes it look better—by leaning upright cards against the tails sticking out from the front and back. You may want to use special cards, like aces of spades, on the outside. Lean a pair of horizontal cards on each side to give the right slope to the base.

2. Roof the column with four cards alternated at right angles. Build two identical pipe columns on the first and you're done. The whole thing is a hair over five feet, seven inches tall and has twenty-eight card stories, including the three pipe columns. The middle, main section could have been taller, but it's recognizable as the New York landmark.

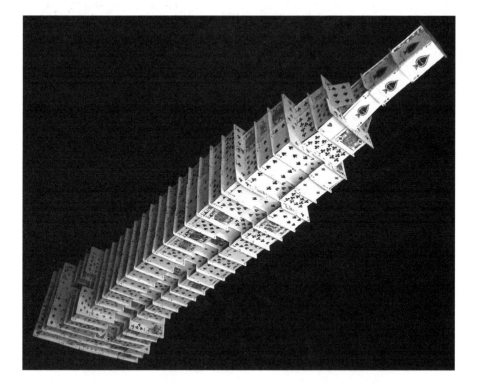

Not Just the Same Old Drill

Oil derricks aren't the most difficult tower variation, but they're close. A derrick is a platform supported by nothing but four thin legs. The legs are like trees, because they start with a pipe column and broaden out. They must be almost perfectly straight.

Oil derricks can be large or small, but I pulled out the stops for this one. The legs alone are sixteen layers tall, including two-story pipe columns at the bottoms. These aren't detailed plans because only seasoned card stackers—or wildcat drillers—will want to take this structure on. It took me about four and a half hours and around fifty-two decks.

Each of the four legs started with a two-story pipe column. Each member had five cards that I prestressed, the way I showed you in Chapter 3. The third layer was a standard cell (made with five cards in each member), but with so little room the tails hung over the edges. I tried to align the horizontal cards with the pipe columns' vertical cards. I also prestressed the horizontal cards by flexing them from side to side instead of top to bottom.

I roofed the cell and built a standard cell with a fence on top of it. The next eleven layers were standard cells with fences and roofs much like the tower at the beginning of this chapter. I used three cards in each member and tried to align the grids. I extended the roof on layer fourteen by putting on a second roof that hung over the edge by about a quarter of an inch. Another standard roof went on top of that. There's nothing structural about the roof edge; it was purely decorative.

I built another standard cell and extended the roof edge again. The last cell in each leg was offset slightly so it was wider, with a smaller center box.

The first few times I made oil derricks, I obsessed about building the legs in exactly the right spots. I built all of them at the same time and spent a lot of time ensuring that they weren't too far apart or too close together. Then I realized I could just move them wherever I wanted. I merely push on the bottom card in the plate supporting the whole thing. It's not hard, if done slowly and gently; just make sure you touch only the bottom card. Do that, and you can move them anywhere.

The legs often lean, so try to place them so that they lean toward one another. Space them closer together if they seem unstable or farther apart if they're strong and true. I try to get them in perfect square and check the space until there's only about a card's length between them at the top.

After the legs were in position, I extended the roof edges with cards laid face down so they'd look better from below.

I bridged the four legs with a solid row of cards across the gaps. That left just a small gap at the center, which I covered with cards laid at an angle.

I added a standard roof and built a grid with double cards on that. I also extended the tails to the edges with added cards. I wanted a low-pitched roof, so I inserted upright cards, then roofed the grid and inserts to make a rail.

I built another grid inside the rail, and a wide-set cell went on top.

Shingles covered all the sides, including the corners. Then I put a final two-story pipe column on the peak.

Some people think these structures resemble Asian temples. I've always called them oil derricks for one reason: That's how a boy at the show where I built the first one described it.

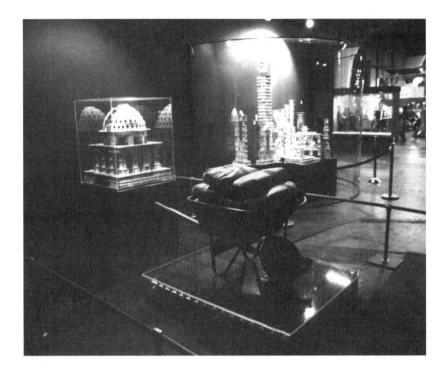

Heavy Duty

- Dome, card city, and weight-bearing grid
- San Francisco, September 2001
- 570 decks
- 35 hours

My project for Exploratorium, the hands-on science museum in San Francisco, stood next to Mathematica, an exhibit that brought math to the masses in the early 1960s. Charles and Ray Eames, a husband-and-wife team famous for innovation, had designed it. Their stackable chairs and molded-plywood chairs are classics. Mathematica was so advanced it's still on display after more than forty years.

It was fitting for the Eameses to build a math exhibit. They manipulated geometry in their designs to create an industrial feel that fit with the 1950s and 1960s.

The couple even designed a deck of cards specifically for building, with slots to lock them together—unlike the standard decks I use.

Architects revere the influential designs of the Eameses, so I was honored to build something in conjunction with Mathematica.

My main project fit with the math theme. It showed how even flimsy materials— such as cards—can be strong when placed in a geometric, repetitive pattern. It was a three-story grid topped with a thick Plexiglas sheet so spectators could look down and see the cards at work.

"When they look, it's sort of floating on cards," said Bryan Connell, the museum's manager of public programs. Each weight-bearing part of the grid was three cards thick for extra strength. I left off the outside wall so visitors could get a better idea of the structure and how repeating the form spreads out the load.

A wheelbarrow holding about six hundred pounds of sand sat atop the Plexiglas. The grid easily could have held a thousand pounds or more, but we limited the load for safety. My only fear was that the wheelbarrow's three points of contact with the surface would distribute the weight unevenly, especially if the Plexiglas flexed. But there was no problem, and the grid remained standing for more than a month, when it finally was dismantled.

Other projects at Exploratorium showed how the same basic structural system can be manipulated for a variety of effects. I built a dome supported by twelve pylons and a city of cards.

Blowing Your Stack

Every one of my card structures meets the same end: I knock it down, destroying hundreds of hours of painstaking work. I do this in part to prove there's nothing holding the cards together. That's especially important when I'm building a record-setting tower: Guinness rules say that the cards cannot be joined in any way.

I also do it because the audience wants it. Spectators want proof that a building really is made only of cards. They deserve to see it come down. After all, a house of cards is by its very nature something temporary.

Demolition also is my reward. All the bits of energy that go into construction—the delicate effort used to put each card in place—are stored in those cards, waiting to be released in a spectacular burst. Putting them together is like executing surgery; taking them down is like detonating dynamite. I can't say I've ever been sad about knocking something down, because building it usually has been a great experience. I love to make card buildings, and I always know I'll do another. That gives me energy.

Some people tell me to ram my fist through the thing I'm demolishing or just kick it over. They don't like waiting as I tinker with it, but taking down a building bit by bit shows an appreciation for it. It's like food: When you see someone wolf down filet mignon or crème brûlée, you wonder what the point was. It's a crime to gobble it without taking time to enjoy it. It's also a shame to demolish in a second a card structure that was built in hours or days.

I recommend knocking down all your card buildings after taking time to show them off, appreciate the work, and take photos. But don't rush it. Playing as you destroy a structure is more fun and educational. Each time you demolish a project you'll also learn something that will help make your next one even better.

I still learn things with each demolition, even after years of building with cards. As I build, I develop a perception of a structure's health and welfare—its capacity for stress and weight. I fret that a slight bump might ruin hours of work. But every time I knock down a building, I realize I was too worried. Demolition has taught me that the structures are sturdier than I think. Even the weakest structure usually is stronger than I believed. That makes it easier for me to build, because I'm not as afraid. Mistakes aren't as likely as I fear, and when they happen they rarely destroy anything.

You'll see this, too, after making several structures. It's liberating to learn that what you're building isn't delicate. Card stacking is more fun when you understand your structures are not brittle leaves, ready to crumble at a touch. Demolishing

them carefully can also teach you how to repair and mold card buildings without breaking them.

A leaf blower is my favorite instrument of destruction. It's noisy, it's windy, and it's controllable. It lets me dissect a building until it dies. As I aim the nozzle, I can see how many walls, floors, or columns must fall before the building collapses. I can see how far it sways before it tips completely. All those things teach me which techniques work best.

If you use a leaf blower or other wind source, aim it away from the building before you turn it on, then slowly point it toward the structure. A tall or slender building usually will sway or bend until it no longer can correct itself and it finally breaks.

My towers sometimes sway by themselves. One twelve-footer I built in the New Orleans Superdome swayed for days—but it didn't fall. It wasn't particularly windy there; it's just that the tall ones have so much surface area that even tiny air currents work in unison to move them. Real buildings react the same way. Anyone who's toured a skyscraper probably has heard that it sways slightly in high winds.

You'll also notice that exterior cards blow off first while interior cards take more force to dislodge. That's because the interior cards are holding the weight. The outer cards are like books on shelves: They aren't what's holding up the whole thing, so they come off easily without a collapse.

You'll see how slab buildings can handle a lot of force on their ends but far less on their sides. That phenomenon shows how a building's footprint affects its structure. A slab is like a person standing with his feet apart: Both are easier to push over from the front or back than from the side. Actual slablike buildings are braced to resist crosswinds because their surface area makes them into huge sails.

Here are some other demolition ideas:

♣ If you don't have a leaf blower or you don't want that kind of power in your living room, try an ordinary house fan. Go from low speed to high and see what kind of force it takes to knock down your building.

♣ You could play Jenga and dissect your building card by card, removing cards until only a few hold up the whole thing. Notice what cards you can extract without causing a total collapse. You'll be surprised at how many you can safely remove. A card sometimes will be hard to pull at first, then suddenly slip out easily because the weight it bore has been transferred to another card. Pull cards from only one side and see how far the building will lean before it falls. Bringing a building to the edge of collapse makes it easy to see which cards really do the work.

♣ Give your building a love tap—a gentle smack. Then tap it progressively harder. Notice how much force it takes to do serious damage or to demolish it.

♣ Pile books, cards, or other weight on a structure. It's surprising how much one will bear before it collapses. You also could "bomb" your structure by dropping objects on it. See what parts can take the most punishment.

♣ Roll something into the building. You could start small, with ball bearings or golf balls, and move up in size until the structure collapses. You might be surprised to see smaller balls punch holes through a building without actually knocking it down.

♣ If you have a baby or toddler in the house, turn her loose on your structure. She's probably been itching to get at the cards anyway, so she'll have a blast tearing into a tower. Be sure to get photos.

♣ Sic the family pet on it. J.R. the cat sometimes is coaxed into the job of demolition supervisor at my house.

♣ Try laying a thread along the edge of a roof deck somewhere near the middle or bottom of a building. Grab both ends and pull the loop of thread through. If you do it right, the structure will survive as the thread slides along under the cards without disturbing them—much like the old trick of yanking a cloth out from under dishes.

In the ten years I've built professionally with cards, I've seen my buildings die in just about every way possible. My first record-setting tower fell only after I sat on the floor and bored a hole through it with my hand. It kind of walked across the floor as it tumbled.

A huge Iowa State Fair crowd gathered when I demolished my card model of the Iowa Capitol, a project that had used two thousand decks. I was amazed to see parts of it survive a leaf blower's full force while others fell instantly. In Copenhagen, two men and I tried to knock down a record-setting tower by jumping onto the platform supporting it. Nothing happened, so we dug into a corner of the tower and pulled out an amazing number of cards before it came down.

In Boston, the former Bruins defenseman Gary Doak used a hockey stick to demolish a card model of the old Boston Garden but left standing my model of the FleetCenter, the arena built to replace it.

A card city I built in the lobby of the Las Vegas Hilton Hotel was hit by an unplanned demolition when someone left a door open. The forty-mile-per-hour gust was strong enough to knock down potted plants and trees besides the finished (thank God) card city.

Other demolitions have been even stranger. The Furniture Guys, Ed Feldman and Joe L'Erario, once picked me up and slammed me headfirst through a tower. The furry Phillie Fanatic baseball mascot destroyed my model of Philadelphia's Veterans Stadium with a belly flop and a kick from his oversize shoe. And in Buffalo, an Elvis impersonator swiveled his hips, crooned a song, and swung a microphone stand into a world-record tower.

German Engineering

- Record-setting tower
- Berlin, November 1999
- Approximately 2,400 decks
- 70 to 80 hours

My latest record-setting tower was nearly twice as tall as my first—twenty-five feet, three and a half inches—and used more than ten times as many cards.

I used so many more cards because a tower's base area grows exponentially as the tower gets taller. The first record setter was four cards square at the base; the latest was eight cards square.

I built my last record holder at a casino, for a German television network. I knew it would be about 130 stories, but unlike when I built my first tower, I was sure I could do it. After building so many big towers, I knew I could make another one; all the techniques and tricks have become second nature to me. Instead of twenty-five feet, it

could have been thirty or fifty, and I think my approach would have been the same.

Construction took more than two weeks of steady work while a camera crew documented every step. The finale—demolition—was a huge production, with

German movie stars, banners, and the works. A makeup artist even followed me around to keep me well powdered during the last few hours. It was out of control.

It was a lot of hoopla, but my first tower—the little, fourteen-and-a-half-foot one—was more satisfying. I didn't really feel like a star in Berlin, despite the attention. In 1992, back in Spirit Lake, Iowa, I felt as if I got my proverbial fifteen minutes of fame—even though the publicity amounted to a newspaper story in the local weekly and pieces on two radio stations.

Don't get me wrong—a twenty-five-foot tower still amazes me, but it wasn't amazing that I could do it. I now see there's no limit to how tall I can build something.

So the next time you pass by a radio mast or television tower, stop for a minute—and imagine it's made of cards.

STACK AWAY

When I started stacking cards, I could hardly get two of them to stand up. It was extremely frustrating, but to me card buildings have always involved a miniature architecture that simply needed some thought. I started stacking at about age eight. By age seventeen I held the world record for tallest card building and was headed to college to study architecture. Not only was card stacking fun, but it had given me a life ambition.

Follow your interests. Recognize your talents and pursue them, regardless of how pointless they *might* seem. Fundamentally, everything we do, every dream, is useful. Don't expect to understand where your talents might take you; just be brave enough to follow them.

For parents, that may mean tolerating a room cluttered with the activities of play and creativity. It's necessary if your children are to grow up and celebrate their individuality. My parents put up with it, even in the living room, for years on end. I thank them for that.

No project is beyond your ability if you practice the techniques in this book, develop techniques of your own, and keep stacking. If you can dream it, chances are you can build it. When you do, visit www.cardstacker.com and email a photo to me, or send it to Bryan Berg, The Cardstacker, P.O. Box 294, Johnston, Iowa 50131-0294.

ABOUT THE AUTHORS

Bryan Berg set his first Guinness World Record for tallest freestanding tower of cards in 1992, when he was seventeen. He has built with cards professionally since 1994 and has appeared in almost every major U.S. city and in Japan, Denmark, and Germany. He has appeared on CBS, ABC, the Discovery Channel, CNN, Fox, and WTBS. Berg earned an architecture degree from Iowa State University in 1997 and later taught architecture there.

Thomas O'Donnell worked as a reporter and editor for the *Des Moines Register* for nearly sixteen years and covered technology, science, and higher education. He left in 2000 to pursue this and other projects. He lives near Des Moines.